D0175009

In Other Words

A Language Lover's Guide to the Most
Intriguing Words Around the World

Christopher J. Moore

Foreword by Simon Winchester

Acknowledgments

Does travel narrow the mind, as the cynical saying goes? Or does it bring you into an endless realm of fun, liveliness, incredulity, and oddities, in the spirit of the Czech proverb, "Each new language offers you another life" (see chapter 2). Risking all, my own life has tended toward the latter, and some of the fruit of these experiences is offered in the following pages. The 250-odd untranslatable words and phrases gathered into this collection, from over 55 countries, are completely random and whimsical, and I have made no attempt whatsoever to be exhaustive in either languages or words. They reflect no more than ideas, concepts, phrases, and sayings, which have at one time or another lodged in a curious mind and made it even more curious.

The words are shown as phonetically pronounced by an English speaker, with the stress shown in italics. Where some compound words, as in German, have two stresses, the first will be the stronger. Some specific vowels and consonants are indicated below.

j- is the French sound j-, a soft, slurred jay.
dj- is the English sound j- in jail.
tch- is the sound ch- in chatter.
ch- or -ch is the sound -ch in Scottish loch.
-onh is the nasal French sound on.
-anh is the nasal French sound in.
-o- is a short -o- as in hot.
-oh- is a long -o- as in comb.
-a- is a short -a- as in fat.
-ay- is the long -a- as in fake.
-ah is a long -a- as in far.
-i is a short -i- as in dip.
-ey- is a long -i- as in hide.

The net must be cast wide for the breadth of information gathered in a book of this kind, and many friends, colleagues, and collaborators have pointed me in useful directions, or given help in specialist areas. I should like to acknowledge gratefully the following contributions and sources as listed below.

Jan Bogaerts for contributions on Dutch life and linguistic inventiveness.
David Bond for problems of cross-cultural translation in "Playing with Words or The Real Fun of Language," *English-Learning and Languages Review*, 1999.

Dr. Qing Cao, Senior Lecturer in Chinese and program leader in Chinese Studies at Liverpool John Moores University, United Kingdom, for his contribution to and clarification of Chinese words.
Chamouni, of ProZ Forums, for

untranslatables from Haitian Creole.
Marc Chavannes for interpreting *gedogen* in "*Gedogen* Allows the Dutch to Manage the Unmanageable," University of California, Berkeley, *Public Affairs Report*, Vol. 41, No. 4, September 2000.

The Copenhagen Post for a colorful explanation of the elusive Danish concept of *hygge* in "Hygge – A nation's defence mechanism?" 8 January, 2004.

Tim Davies, freelance translator specializing in Danish, Norwegian, and Swedish, for his contribution of Swedish and Danish words.

Rose del Castillo Guilbault for her thoughts on the misunderstandings surrounding *macho* in "Untranslatable Words: 'Macho,'" Ponencias Instituto Cultural "Raíces Mexicanas," 1996.

Thomas G. Dineen III for reflections on the Greek quality of *thymos* in "Cultural Conservatism, a compendium of traditionalist thought on politics, literature, the fine arts, and other matters," www.culturalconservatism.org

R.M.W. Dixon for his scholarship on Australian indigenous languages in *The Languages of Australia*, St. Lucia: Cambridge University Press, 1980.

Graham Dunstan Martin for thoughts on French untranslatability.

Eddy Echternach for a Web window into the mind of the Dutch, www.eddyechternach.nl

Elvin Geng for his article "What's In a Word – U.S.-China Relations Built on a Frail Bridge of Language," *Pacific News Service*, February 1998.

Juan Goytisolo for his article "Jemâa-el-Fna's thousand and one nights," *The Courier*, Unesco, December 2000.

David C. Gross for his entertaining *English-Yiddish Dictionary*, Hippocrene Books, New York, 1995.

Andrew Horvat, *Japanese Beyond Words: How to Walk and Talk like a Native Speaker*, California: Stone Bridge Press, 2000.

Thomas Hylland Eriksen for insights into Scandinavian nationalities in "Images of the neighbour, reciprocal national stereotypes in Scandinavia," 1997, folk.uio.no/geirthe/Scandinavian_images.html

Yelena Kalashnikova for material from an interview titled "'There are no good and bad translators. There are only felicitous and infelicitous translations' But only a good translator can produce a felicitous translation" with the translator Vladimir Muravyov in *The Russian Journal*, 16 July 2001.

Tim Kirk for background on German political language, in his thorough and illuminating *Dictionary of Modern German History*, Cassell, 2002.

Boyé Lafayette De Mente for his words about *yoko meshi* in *The Japanese Have a Word for It*, Chicago: Passport Books, 1994.

Dominik Lukeš for his article explaining the idiosyncracies of the Czech language in "Czech Language Inside Out," www.bohemica.com

Christian Maclean for interpretations of the German notion of *Gemut*.

Joumana Medlej for interesting observations on Arabic culture in "Thinking about Tongues," www.cedarseed.com/air/blabla3.html

Ineke Mok and **Peter Reinsch** for explaining the Dutch term *medelander*

in *Handbook for International Teaching Materials*, Utrecht: Parel, 1999.

Alain Nicollier for his comprehensive *Dictionnaire des mots suisses*, Geneva: Editions GVA, 1990.

Nigel Pennick for thoughts on Norse traditions from *Rune Magic: The History and Practice of Ancient Runic Traditions*, New York: HarperCollins, 1993.

Stephen Ryan, Eichi University for cross-cultural issues in Russian and English, reporting from the 1998 TESOL Russia–Far East International Conference, September 22–24, 1998, Khabarovsk, Russia, *The Language Teacher*, January 1999.

David Shyovitz for background in "The History and Development of Yiddish," *Jewish Virtual History*, 2003.

Tang Si Xian in Taiwan for insights into daily life in Chinese society.

Jeffrey Tayler for reflections on the uncertainties in Russian life in "Searching for equanimity in the skies above Siberia," *Atlantic Monthly*, February, 2001.

Daryl Taylor, licensed translator of Finnish into English, for his contribution and clarification of Finnish untranslatables.

Albert Valdman for background on Creole and pidgin in *Le Créole*, Paris: Editions Klincksieck, 1978.

Dragan Velikic˘ for an extract from "Budapest, Strictly Personal," translated by Marco Ivic˘, *The Hungarian Quarterly*, Vol. 41, No. 157, October 1999.

Christina Waters for thoughts on the word *terrior*, quoted in Frank Galuszka's "The Palette as a System," *Proceedings of the American Society for Cybernetics 2001 Conference*,

Vancouver, May 2001.

Alan Watts for his insightful *Tao: The Watercourse Way*, edited by Al Huang, New York: Pantheon, 1975.

Brian Whitaker, Middle East editor, for insights into Arabic creativity in "What's in a word?," *The Guardian*, 25 August, 2000.

Olga T. Yokoyama for the untranslatability of Russian humor in *The Russian Context*, Eloise M. Boyle & Genevra Gerhart, eds., Slavica, reviewed in *Russian Life*, January/February 2003.

Dr. Henry Zhao, Modern Chinese Reader, the School of Oriental and Asian Studies, University of London, for his contribution to the Chinese section introduction.

The publisher would also like to thank the following people for their contributions to this book: Anna Amari-Parker, Zhaleh Beheshti, Emma Britton, Louise Chung, Fred Ciporen, Sharanjit Dhol, Ramazan Durak, Agnieszka Forsen, Takuya Fujiyoshi, George Gibson, Timan Janke, Gunnel Klingener, Elliot Langford, Jacek Lentz, Louie Menashe, and Angela Smith.

Every effort has been made to obtain permissions for material used in this book and to contact the copyright holders. The publishers apologize for any omissions and would welcome contact from copyright holders for correction in subsequent editions.

Contents

" . . . being exposed to the existence of other languages increases the perception that the world is populated by people who not only speak differently from oneself but whose cultures and philosophies are other than one's own. Perhaps travel cannot prevent bigotry but by demonstrating that all peoples cry, laugh, eat, worry and die, it can introduce the idea that if we try to understand each other, we may even become friends.

Maya Angelou,
*Wouldn't Take Nothing
for My Journey Now*

Foreword

Simon Winchester

I rather suspect that when Sofia Coppola made her movie *Lost in Translation*, she prayed that it might turn out to be, if nothing else, a *succès d'estime*. Had that turned out to be true, her hopes would have had a nicely linguistic irony all of their own, since the French phrase is barely translatable itself, and refers to a phenomenon – an artistic creation unlikely to make much money but loved by the wiser critics – that, incredibly, is matched by no handy off-the-shelf equivalent word in this oh-so-flexible and oh-so-enormous lexicon that we are proud to trumpet as English.

In the end, her film, which was variously described as haunting, elegiac, and touchingly memorable, turned out to be a huge commercial triumph, probably hauling in more dollars per day than any of her father's productions. And while some of us who enjoy non-English phrases because they are often so elegant, succinct, and uniquely employable, may have been briefly regretful not to be able to employ the aforementioned *succès* in this case, her film briefly turned the spotlight on another inescapable, but often overlooked, reality. People who are not us – or *foreigners*, which of course includes *us* in *their* eyes too – speak, write, and do things that are alien, mysterious, and impossibly difficult to translate, but which, when explained, often make an awful lot of sense.

And further: The moment you understand the words and phrases and the wonderfully sensible concepts that they frequently encapsulate, you have come some small way toward understanding the people who employ them. Which, it seems to me, is the prime benefit (aside from the serendipitous pleasures of browsing) of the delightful treasure-house – literally the *thesaurus* – of linguistic marvels that follows.

Take the Chinese word *mianzi*, for example. Having no other word to use, we call this "face," and it represents, very roughly, *the inner dignity that is possessed by every human, which all others dealing with its possessor are duty bound to uphold, and neither to threaten nor to challenge.* Shout an insult at a Chinese shopkeeper and you make him *lose face*, you threaten his *mianzi*, and you commit the most cardinal of sins. Buy your Chinese colleague the most expensive cognac imaginable and you *give him face*, and you will in consequence be blessed for all eternity.

Having lived in China for many years, I had long supposed the East to be more richly endowed with untranslatable and lexically inscrutable concepts, such as *mianzi*, than any other part of the world. That was until recently, when I met a young Russian student in California. This woman, now a hopeless convert to the joys of English, had as a child been very skeptical about its merits: Yes, she said, there were pleasing enough words in English – she mentioned *melancholy*, *sequester*, and *mandolin* for starters. But why, she asked, was there no single word in English for concepts that in Russian are so simple? Why nothing for *country house*? Or for *smoked fish*? To her, English had been merely a stiff and functional language: The Russian she had spoken as a child – and what is revealed in the following pages (with Russian words like *razbliuto*: do please look it up) – is in many ways as she suggested: infinitely richer, more romantic, and filled with very un-English cadence and with possibility.

In defense of the fugitive wonders of the English to which my student was initially blind, I have always enjoyed our tongue's singular oddities – such as, *mallemaroking*, a word that was once defined as *the carousing of drunken sailors on icebound Greenland whaling ships* and one that seems a perfect example of the remarkably inclusive nature of the tongue we speak. (The definition has lately changed, omitting the word "Greenland," indicating, no doubt, the globalizing of the *mallemarokers'* habit.) But Christopher Moore will no doubt chide me gently, or reprove me (debates about this particular usage further reminds me of the pleasures of English), by suggesting that however inclusive English may well be, speakers in the outside world can always show us how much more subtly so their languages can manage to be.

And then I find myself drifting dreamily in agreement with him, back to my beloved East, and wondering, indeed, how on Earth it can be that we speak a language that has no equivalent for the most subtly delicious of all Japanese phrases: *mono-no-aware*, which means no more and no less than *appreciating the sadness of existence*. You see the cherry blossoms on the trees in Kyoto in April and you love them, but you love them most of all because you appreciate, so sadly, that soon they will all be gone. *Mono-no-aware*: a phrase, which like all Japanese words has every syllable pronounced, which deserves never to be lost in translation, and which serves as a reminder that the understanding of tongues other than our own offers us a chance to come to a better understanding of peoples other than ourselves – an understanding that can only be for the betterment of us all.

Introduction

 t is 1939 and two Finnish foot soldiers are pinned down in a battle during the war between Finland and Russia.

"We're outnumbered," one soldier says. "There must be over forty of them, and only two of us."

"Dear God, it'll take us all day to bury them!" exclaims the other.

Finnish people tell this story, along with a variety of others, to illustrate the national characteristic known as *sisu*. *Sisu,* says Professor Kate Remlinger, linguist at Grand Valley State University, is an untranslatable word, meaning something like a dogged and proud refusal to lie down and be beaten. "The way people talk is a reflection of their worldview, their history, and their upbringing," she says, observing that the idea of *sisu* is so important to the Finns that, three generations after emigrating to the United

States of America, it continues to infuse local Michigan dialect and culture.

In the 1940s, Benjamin Lee Whorf introduced the theory that language proceeds from and shapes our cultural life in *Language, Thought, and Reality*. Whorf's research into the speech and culture of the Hopi Indians, whose language, like Chinese, has no concept of tenses, started a wave of enquiry into the relationship between language and culture. Academics refer to this area of study as "sociolinguistics." What emerges is not only the universal phenomenon that certain languages have "no word for X" – such as the widely held notion that the Inuit peoples have no word for "snow," and the more significant fact that the Algonquin people have no word for "time" – but also, conversely, that languages, indeed whole cultures, have words, terms, and ideas that are simply untranslatable.

Of course we borrow words like mad when it suits us, when we have no equivalent in our own tongue. Modern languages are like archaeological digs once we begin to explore where many of our words in daily use come from. Brian Whitaker, the Middle Eastern correspondent of the British newspaper, *The Guardian,* once provided a list of some eighty common English words and asked which one was the odd man out:

admiral, alchemy, alcohol, alcove, algebra, algorithm,
alkali, almanac, amalgam, aniline, apricot, arsenal,
arsenic, artichoke, assassin, aubergine, azure, borax,
cable, calibre, camphor, candy, cannabis, carafe, carat,
caraway, checkmate, cipher, coffee, cotton, crimson,
crocus, cumin, damask, elixir, gauze, gazelle, ghoul,
giraffe, guitar, gypsum, hashish, hazard, jar, jasmine,
lacquer, lemon, lilac, lime, lute, magazine, marzipan,
massage, mattress, muslin, myrrh, nadir, orange,
safari, saffron, samizdat, sash, sequin, serif, sesame,
shackle, sherbet, shrub, sofa, spinach, sugar, sultana,
syrup, talc, tamarind, tambourine, tariff, tarragon,
zenith, zero.

The answer, of course, is *samizdat,* an untranslatable Russian word meaning "underground dissident writing." The rest are all Arabic words that, during the seven centuries of Islamic occupation of Spain, Portugal, and parts of southern France, were equally untranslatable. Western mathematicians, for instance, had no idea of the concept of "zero" until Arab terminology gave it to them, along with *algebra* and *algorithm.* Arab astrologers taught us *zenith* and *nadir,* while *massage, sherbet, hashish,* and *sofa* introduced us to a sensuality of which God-fearing crusaders had never even dreamed.

But back to *samizdat* and our own times. When, in 1986, the then Soviet president Mikhail Gorbachev announced the new policy of *perestroika* – the age of *glasnost* began and the age of *samizdat* ended. How else is one supposed to say this without several paragraphs of commentary on Russian cultural history? Of course we may agree on, "When the Soviet government introduced its program of economic and social reforms and relaxed its grip on freedom of speech, the period of underground dissident writing came to an end." But does that language indicate the true flavor of the years of struggle toward democracy in Communist Russia? In those years, *samizdat* became a cultural phenomenon, representing rebellion and creativity, laced with danger and heroism. *Glasnost,* the idea of openness, was an almost unimaginable change when it came on the scene and, together with *perestroika,* was the harbinger of the end of Communism, the collapse of the Soviet Union, the end of the Cold War, the fall of the Berlin Wall, and repercussions that we are still living through today. All three terms have now entered English as concepts for which we had, and still have, no equivalent translation.

It is easy to imagine how confusion arises and even marvel how more doesn't, especially in politics, when trying to cross an untranslatable gap. When Jiang Zemin, the Chinese president at that time, visited the United States of America in 1997, he caused a lot of fuss by suggesting that the idea of "democracy" originated 2,000 years ago with Chinese philosophers. Liberal American commentators thought this absurd. But as Elvin Geng, a graduate in Asian Studies, points out:

> The word *minzhu* first appeared in a classic work
> called *Shuji* where it referred to a benevolent "ruler
> of the people," that is, a leader whose legitimacy
> rests on the people's welfare. Those who ruled by
> force and oppression, in contrast, were not given
> this title.
>
> In the late nineteenth century, *minzhu* was the
> word used to translate "democracy" – in Chinese,
> the one term can mean "rule of the people" as well
> as "ruler of the people."
>
> Both uses of *minzhu* share the sense that the
> government ought to operate to meet the needs
> of the people. This criterion may be fulfilled by
> an enlightened dictator or a Leninist regime as
> well as by a U.S.-style constitutional democracy.

From words that mean something quite different, to words that don't exist. No word for "snow" in the Inuktitut language of the Alaskan region? The truth is there are too many words, shades of meaning that a generic word cannot quantify. Just as in English we have snowstorm, flurry, drift, bank, flake, and fall.

Perhaps more of a concern is that the Japanese language apparently has no word for "water." Or more precisely, *mizu,* the word for water, actually means "cold water" as opposed to *oyu,* "hot water." It's possible that, for the Japanese, hot and cold water must be so different that they cannot be grouped under the same word. You might just as well say, as Alice's Mad Hatter argued, that there is no resemblance between hot coffee and cold coffee. Come to think of it, maybe the Japanese are on to something.

We suppose that most experiences are common and translatable between different cultures, but this simply isn't so.

Take a closer look at the word "dreaming." What are we to make of the fact that languages such as Spanish and Italian have the same noun for "sleep" as for "dream," while others, like French and English, differentiate between the two? Do some nations sleep differently from others? What we mean by "dreaming" is plainly not the same as what the speakers of Aranda, an indigenous language of central Australia, mean when they say *aljerre*. For Indigenous Australians, dreaming is a vital way of holding the created world together. British author Bruce Chatwin writes, "Aboriginal myths tell of the legendary totemic beings who wandered across the country in the Dreamtime . . . singing the world into existence." If a tribe's Keeper of the Dreaming fails to carry out his or her "dreaming" task, walking the songlines that put the world together, the Earth as we know it will come to an end.

We would have the same difficulty trying to get an Irishman to say "yes" or "no." If you have ever wondered why those Irish plays are full of replies such as "It is," "I do," and "I am not," it is because the Irish tongue simply does not have the words "yes" and "no." Does it? It does not. Do you think this is strange? I do. Are you perplexed? Indeed I am.

When we get into information technology, of course, the entire world bows to English – "Internet," "Web," "surf," "click" – transmogrified into local forms such as *surfer* (French) and *surfear* (Spanish), *cliquer* and *cliquear*. An earlier generation had the same problem with "telephone." When the Arabic language, for instance, had to choose between the pure and poetic *al-hatif,* a classical word meaning, literally, "the invisible caller" or the more blatant borrowing *al-talafoon*, the latter naturally went on to become the everyday word.

With unbridgeable gaps at such a basic level, how much more untranslatable are higher insights or realizations attained only through a lifetime's discipline and practice? Experiences on this level are no longer commonplace and most of us can only guess at their meaning. An example is *e-ma-ho,* an untranslatable Tibetan word expressing the sense of wonder and awe that arises

when one truly comes to know reality. Oriental philosophy and
spirituality are full of such terms, creating a huge problem for
the translators of Eastern texts. Alan Watts, the great exponent
of Taoism in the West, spent a lifetime trying to get across the
concepts of the Tao and, in writing his last book, tried for one last
time to break through the barrier of untranslatability by literally
renouncing the attempt to explain Taoism intellectually. His
friend and collaborator Al Chung-Liang Huang remembers:

> During our last semester . . . at the finish of an
> afternoon session when the high-flying spirit
> had set everyone smiling, dancing, and
> rolling up and down the grassy slopes,
> Alan and I started to walk back to
> the lodge, feeling exuberant. Alan
> turned to me and started to speak.
> I noticed a sudden breakthrough
> in his expression, a look of
> lightness and glow appeared
> all around him. Alan had
> discovered a different way to
> tell me of his feelings: "Yah
> . . . Ha . . . Ho . . . Ha! Ho
> . . . La Cha Om Ha . . .
> Deg deg te te . . . Ta de de
> ta te ta . . . Ha te te Ha
> hom . . . Te Te Te. . . ."
> We gibbered and danced
> all the way up the hill. Everyone around
> understood what we were saying. Alan knew, too,
> that he had never – not in all his books – said it any
> better than that.

If only it were as easy to get across the idea behind the English
word "cool." Cool is universally just cool, man.

~ Chapter 1 ~

Western European Languages

E urope is a continent now dedicated to the very principle of "living together" – a plain and easily translatable notion, one would have thought. But in reality this simple idea wends its way through many different meanings, connotations, and associations across the continent.

The various takes on the idea of "living together" across European languages throw into relief the difficulties of translating an idea that may have hugely diverse implications in different cultures. In Britain, for example, where an Englishman's house is his castle and it is possible to live for years without knowing your neighbors, the phrase "living together" refers without ambiguity to the domestic arrangement of unmarried couples. But how do we translate that particular meaning in Spain, a country where unmarried couples represent a relatively new phenomenon in post-Franco society?

In Spain, the word *convivencia* alludes to "living together with others," the quality of a society where citizens get along by practicing tolerance and mutual respect. In this sense, it comes close to meaning a "civic culture," a notion that Britons would struggle to come to terms with.

Perhaps the English term "cohabit" might help to shed some light on the problem? Perhaps not. Cross to France and *cohabitation* has a very specific political use, meaning a coalition in government between normally irreconcilable parties who are making an effort to exercise power together. As for personal cohabitation, French gives us the nice old expression *être marié de la main gauche,* but in their abstractly precise way they also have the modern provisions of the *loi du concubinage* for unmarried

couples "living together." It goes without saying that if you called a woman a "concubine" in Britain, it would not be very well received.

Germany throws its hat in the ring with the word *zusammenleben*. Differing from the much warmer Spanish *convivencia,* the *zusammenleben* idea of "living together" is a more pragmatic notion of "getting along" in your family or in the community. Again, like the Spanish, it has nothing to do with actually living with someone, which is expressed most soulfully and emotionally by *Lebensgefährte* or *Lebensgefährtin,* "the one who travels life's road with you." However, times being what

they are, and relationships more transient, a commonly heard term nowadays is *Lebensabschnittsgefährte* – "a bit of life companion." Only German, with its processional word joining, could come up with such a creation!

These days in Holland *samenwonen,* "living together," is a neutral term in every sense, but only a generation ago unmarried couples were said to *hokken,* literally, "live in a pigpen together."

And what of *verzuiling,* a much used word in the Dutch idea of living together? This literally means "compartmentalization" but refers to the highly complex system in Dutch society that allows every minority shade of opinion to be represented and create its own space. This right to one's own space is exercised in all aspects of society: political parties, schools, and so on, creating a patchwork system that for the outsider, or incomer, is very hard to understand.

Moving south to explore the Italian view of "living together," we find that the concept of "partnership" is impossible to express in Italian without much circumlocution. Robert Ardrey, a popular writer on anthropology, once described how Italian society worked through the mechanism of *nodi,* which literally means "knots." *Nodi* are the ties that connect you, and traditionally this means blood ties. In practical terms, if you want to get something done in Italy, like having a new telephone connection installed, it helps if you know someone who knows someone who has an uncle or a cousin in the telephone company. Then you go along with your intermediary and meet the uncle or the cousin in order to explain your problem. After this, your new phone line (for which you have been waiting at least six months) is installed within the week. Ardrey argues that the idea of the common good is practically unknown in Italy, and that Italian society is made up of individuals whose moral values belong first and foremost to families.

In a nice illustration of this *familismo,* the importance of families, David Bond, writing in *English Learning and Languages Review,* describes playing a game with an international group of friends, all living and working in a foreign country at the time. The idea was for each member of the group to think up one word that for them summed up their faraway homeland.

My Italian friend, Saverio, had no doubts. His word, pronounced with dramatic emphasis and not the slightest hesitation, was *tavola.* The thought of an Englishman, or even an Englishwoman, far from

home, murmuring "table" to him or herself in
a tone of wistful longing in the small wee hours
of the morning was totally ludicrous. Yet I knew
exactly what Saverio meant . . . Table has
implications for an Italian, and in Italian, that
it does not have for the English or in English.
It speaks of aspects of family life and of good
fellowship, of mealtimes both as rituals and as
celebrations, of a whole world of food-preparation
and kitchen conversation and of all sorts of other
things that only an Italian could justly describe. The
word for Saverio conjured up a whole universe.

And what was the word that for Bond himself summed up
his homeland? His spontaneous choice was the word "privacy," an
almost diametrically opposed notion of "living together." Back to
the castle.

French

F or many, learning French is plagued by the awareness that however something is expressed in English, inevitably it will come out quite the opposite in French. So the English "taking French leave" results predictably in the Gallic tongue as *filer à l'anglaise*. "Walking up and down" emerges as *marcher de bas en haut*. And so on.

Frecnh, as we will see, is an international language spoken in Belgium, Switzerland, and Canada, quite apart from a host of African and Caribbean countries where it also feeds into Creole and pidgin varieties. Once the universal tongue of refined society and diplomacy, French is also full of richly vulgar and untranslatable slang that can stop foreigners in their tracks. What are we to make of *Il a le cul bordé de nouilles*, literally, "His backside is fringed with noodles"? Would you imagine for a moment that this describes someone who is incredibly lucky? Here are some other Gallicisms that defy translation.

chichi [*shee* shee] (adjective)

English has borrowed this sweet-sounding word as a qualified adjective – we always say, "It's *a bit* chichi" – suggesting something that is "fussily decorated," rather "twee" in style, and reminiscent of the camp world of *La Cage aux Folles*. It's a perfect word for describing someone's interior *décor* that has been arrived at with great effort but with no taste. In the original French, however, *chichi* is a noun meaning more or less "a fuss," and *chercher des chichis* means "to look for unnecessary complications in something."

horripiler [orr-*ee*-pee-lay] (verb)

Untranslatable only in its wonderful brevity, this ghostly sounding word derived straight from the Latin *horrere pilus* means "to make your hair stand on end."

rire jaune [reer *johne*] (idiom)

Literally, "to laugh yellowly," this expression is full of nuances that are hard to translate. As in other cultures, yellow is not a positive color in French, but *un jaune* doesn't mean "a coward" as in English, but rather "a traitor." Yellow is the color of Judas. To *rire jaune* is therefore to give a laugh that betrays your true feelings – a forced or insincere laugh. It betrays you in trying to betray the other.

esprit de l'escalier [es-pree de less-*kal*-iay] (idiom)

A witty remark that occurs to you too late, literally on the way down the stairs. *The Oxford Dictionary of Quotations* defines *esprit de l'escalier* as, "An untranslatable phrase, the meaning of which is that one only thinks on one's way downstairs of the smart retort one might have made in the drawing room."

une quine-mine [oohn keen-*meen*] (noun)

This is a mocking gesture made by placing your thumb on one cheek and flapping the open hand. Not to be practiced by innocents abroad, for fear of the consequences.

sans-culottes [sonh ku-*lott*] (idiom)

Literally, "without breeches," this is the name given to a political movement that played a significant role in the French Revolution and in later social reform movements. In my youthful reading of *The Scarlet Pimpernel,* I was always puzzled as to why sections of the French public walked around with no breeches on. So to explain, the term refers

to a disparate social group made up of artisans, shopkeepers, and lower middle-class republicans who were united only in their hatred of the rich. The name came from the fact that the better-off members refused to wear breeches, which were associated with the aristocracy, and instead went about in trousers, the traditional dress of the working man.

la pedze [lah *pedz*] (adjective)

Coming from the Swiss patois word for "resin" or "glue," this descriptive word refers to someone who stays too long in one place, or to someone who cannot drag themselves from the table after a meal, and especially to a guest who long overstays his welcome. *"C'est la pedze!"*

terroir [terr-*wah*] (noun)

One cannot speak of untranslatable French culture without a nod to viniculture, itself a profoundly mysterious business, full of nuances and shades. *Terroir,* Christina Waters tells us, is "what informs the bouquet and flavor notes of wines . . . a heady confluence of elements that taken together inform the final product. The term indicates that mixture of soil, climate, temperature, geographical location (e.g. longitude, latitude, altitude), possibly even lunar cycle which express themselves in the finished product. Here culture and agriculture meet in the sensory signature of a glass of wine." It could not be said more simply.

demi-monde [de-mee *monhd*] (noun)

A half world, hidden from the mainstream and usually kept secret. It can describe a group of people on the political or legal margins of society, and is particularly used to describe prostitutes and kept women. The Japanese term for this is "the floating world," as described by Kazuo Ishiguro in his novel of the same name.

avoir la molle [a-*vwah* lah *moll*] (idiom)

"To have the molle" is a Swiss idiom that refers to a kind of heavy lethargy that residents along Lake Geneva *(Lac*

Léman) regularly suffer from. It invades them with a listless unwillingness to do any work. Whether the complaint is purely climatic or has something to do with the "day after" feeling that follows a feast day is kept deliberately ambiguous. In local language *une patte-molle,* meaning "a soft foot" is someone with no energy or character – certainly not the common image of the Swiss!

bête noire [bett *nwahr*] (noun)

This vivid expression, literally meaning "black beast," is used all around the world to indicate something or someone that is especially detestable. It can also mean a scapegoat and has a certain frankness and boldness, calling a spade a spade.

enfant terrible [*onh*-fonh terr-*ee*-bler] (noun)

This sounds as if it should mean a "dreadful child" but the phrase nowadays has little or nothing to do with children. It means someone who extravagantly defies convention, usually arising out of a cultural group or movement where the person has a provocative role. Jean Cocteau's 1929 novel *Les Enfants Terribles* describes an adolescent boy confined to a bedroom on account of a head injury, playing out a world of surrealistic fantasies with his sister as they become more and more obsessed with each other. Twenty years later, casting convention to the winds, Jean-Pierre Melville's groundbreaking film of the book is thought to have set the tone for the radical student movements of the Sixties. Both Cocteau and Melville were clearly *enfants terribles.*

intellectuel [anh-tell-ect-u-*ell*] (noun)

Linguists have a term for words known as "false friends." These are words that seem to translate with no problem and then turn out to have quite different associations in another culture. Graham Dunstan Martin points out the untranslatability of the seemingly transparent *intellectuel.* To the French, this word embodies admiration. In British and American culture, anything that smacks of being "clever" is regarded with suspicion. Equally, he says, "there's no French word for 'clever' with just that note of contempt . . . and a sense of not having one's feet on ordinary solid ground . . . Clever, yes, but not solid or reliable, is the implication."

jolie-laide [*jol*-ee-layd] (idiom)

Only the French would have such a way to describe beauty. A wonderful slang expression, it literally means "pretty and ugly" but describes the type of feminine beauty that is human, and not manufactured by plastic surgeons. It's a kind of fascinating quirkiness implying charisma, a face you want to keep looking at, even if you can't decide whether it is beautiful or not.

froufrou [*froo*-froo] (adjective)

A rustling, especially that of a woman's skirt, one of the nicest onomatopoeic words around. This lovely word evokes the whole *risqué* world of *thés dansants, soirées intimes,* and that institution of the discreet venue, the *chambre separée.* There is no way to imagine these delights other than in French.

pièce de résistance [pee-*ess* de ray-ziss-*tonss*] (idiom)

This idiom literally means "a piece of stamina," and it originally referred to the main course of a dinner – the test of your stomach's stamina. In both languages, it now describes an outstanding accomplishment or the final part of something, whether a work of art, a project, or a meal.

métro-boulot-dodo [*me*-tro *boo*-lo *doh*-doh] (idiom)

A star among phrases for an untranslatable succinctness that sums up a pointless existence (subway, work, sleep). The full line of the original poem titled *Couleurs d'usine* by Pierre Béarn is even more eloquent:

Métro boulot bistrots mégots dodo zéro
"Subway work bars fags sleep nothing"

laissez-faire [*lay*-say fahr] (adjective)

This term, with its roots in nineteenth-century trade and politics, has come to suggest any liberal attitude bordering on permissiveness. "He's a bit *laissez-faire* with his children," one might say of a parent who allows a free rein. While the original sense expressed not much more than a kind of noninterventionism, maybe nowadays there is more than a hint of disapproval in the term, a suggestion of indifference.

glauque [glohke] (noun)

The French language has a bountiful supply of color words, including many literary terms where the true meaning is more or less lost. Among my favorites is the atmospherically nasty *glauque,* a word that used to mean "sea-green" but has acquired a kind of unhealthy troubling quality. Jean Cocteau is reputed to have said of the Russian ballet master Diaghilev that he had *"un regard glauque, un regard d'huitre,"* that is, "the eye of an oyster." I think that says it all.

sang-froid [sonh-fr*wah*] (noun)

The English expression "in cold blood" does not come close to the French meaning of *sang-froid,* which is an ability to maintain one's cool. Most often used to describe someone able to perform under great pressure or in great danger, it refers to cold-blooded animals that can stay motionless for long periods of time.

German

H ere is a language with more than its fair share of
untranslatable terms. In areas such as philosophy and
psychology, German culture has often led the way, giving us
ideas from *Gestalt* to *Weltanschauung*. German philosophical
literature is full of powerful and pithy sentences, such as German
dramatist, Gottold Lessing's famous dictum, *"Niemand muss
müssen,"* literally "No-one must 'must.'" German poetry, too,
is among the most intense and untranslatable in the world. In
short, it seems that German thought and language is an amazing
mixture of technical precision and soulful ineffability, which
sparks off a rich creativity in concepts.

But there is at least one basic and practical reason for German's
neologistic tendencies – its limitless capacity for creating new
terms by joining a whole lot of old words together. Words of this
compound type can be richly expressive, and here are some other
untranslatable products of the imaginative German mind.

doppelgänger [dop-ple-*geng*-er] (noun)

Literally a "double goer," the *Doppelgänger* of legend was one's
ghostly shadow-self. This spooky creature lurked at your rear,
cast no reflection, and only you could see it. The English got
hold of the word in the mid-nineteenth century and set about
bastardizing it. Nowadays, it's more or less synonymous
with "lookalike."

torschlusspanik [*toor*-shloos-pahn-*ik*] (noun)

This word is literally translated as "door-shutting panic" and
it captures the anxiety sometimes felt by unmarried females
when they see the shelf and themselves on it. Once upon a
time, the sensation could grip one as young as twenty-one,
but with today's career-focused women deciding to delay
childbirth, *Torschlusspanik* now refers more commonly to
the race against the biological clock.

drachenfutter
[*drack*-uhn-foot-er]
(noun)
Meaning "dragon fodder," this
is the offering German husbands
make to their wives – breathing
raging fire at the cave entrance –
when they've stayed out late or
they have otherwise engaged
in some kind of inappropriate
behavior. A nice box of chocolates, or
some flowers, perhaps to mask
the beer fumes.

schadenfreude [*shar*-den-*froi*-da] (noun)
A compound word consisting of *Schaden* meaning "damage"
and *Freude* meaning "joy." This is a dirty, cackle-rousing kind
of happiness derived from someone else's misfortune. We're
all disgustingly guilty of enjoying this emotion at some time
or other.

zeitgeist [*zeyt*-geyst] (noun)
The "spirit of the time" is much easier to define in
retrospect. Fashion designers do their best to capture it
in decor; newspaper columnists attempt to sum it up;
politicians strive to capitalize on it. In reality, only seriously
hip celebrities manage the ultimate – to surf the *Zeitgeist*.

korinthenkacker [core-*in*-ten-*cuck*-er] (noun)
A "raisin pooper" – that is, someone so taken up with life's
trivial detail that they spend all day crapping raisins. You
can spot these types a mile off – it's that irritating pen pusher
or filing fanatic whose favorite job is tidying up the
stationery cupboard.

gemüt [gem-*ooht*] (noun)
Many visitors to Germany have come across the proudly
claimed adjective *gemütlich,* often translated as "cozy," "snug,"

and "comfortable." Although, to judge from their tourist brochures, the Viennese would like to make the term all their own, *Gemütlichkeit* remains a widely familiar German concept. Harder, if not impossible, to translate, is the root word *Gemüt* with its elusive variety of meanings around the notions of soul, mind, heart, feeling, disposition, nature, and turn of mind. There are a number of good phrases such as *Er hat kein Gemüt* – "he has no feelings," or "he is heartless"; *das deutsche Gemüt* – "the German mentality"; and *ein schlichtes Gemüt* – "a simple soul." From the same elusive root we get *gemütskrank* – "mentally or emotionally disturbed"; *Gemütsruhe* – "peace of mind"; and *gemütsvoll* – "full of feeling, emotional, warmhearted, sentimental." To discover its roots, let's hark back to the impoverished period directly after the Napoleonic wars, when simple pleasures were especially valued in Germany. Imagine a man of later years in a comfortable armchair, accessorized by pipe, slippers, and a warm fire – that's the heart of *gemütlich*.

geisterfahrer [*guy*-ste-fah-rer] (noun)

A compound term again, literally "ghost-driver," meaning a driver who mysteriously appears on the wrong side of the road. While admiring the inventiveness of the word, we may wonder why this phenomenon seems so common on German roads and autobahns?

schnappszahl [*shnapp*-tzahl] (noun)

This is a number that has some striking pattern, whether a date or any combination of figures with an unexpected symmetry. An example would be someone's birthdate being 04-04-44, a palindromic date such as 03-11-30, or a price tag on a garment of 19.91 Euros. No suggestion of luck seems intended.

bildungsroman [*bill*-dungs-roh-mahn] (noun)

This compound word derives from *Bildung*, "education," and *Roman*, "novel." It describes a typically German type of novel, such as Thomas Mann's *The Magic Mountain*, which explores a character's inner development in all its aspects: moral, spiritual, intellectual, and psychological.

politologie [*poll*-ee-toll-ogh-*ee-er*] (noun)

The study of politics, literally, "politology," a term that ought to exist in English, but doesn't. Instead we have the oddly termed "political science," which suggests either that science can be politicized, or that politics can be scientific. Either proposition is rather worrying.

nesthocker [*nest*-hok-er] (noun)

This word was originally a biological sciences word used when observing the behavior of birds leaving the nest to fly. More recently, it has come to refer to a person who stays at home, rather than moving out and finding their own feet – the thirty–eight–year–old who is still living at home with Mom and Dad.

weltschmerz [*velt*-shmairtz] (noun)

This is a compound word consisting of *Welt,* meaning "world," and *Schmerz,* meaning "pain." Just as your head can hurt *(Kopfschmerzen),* or you can suffer from a stomachache, *(Magenschmerzen),* so the world can hurt too. In its mildest form, this is "world-weariness." At the other extreme, it's an existential pain that leaves you reeling with a damaging, head-clutching despair.

Italian

T o Italians, the best-known poem of modern times was written by Giuseppe Ungaretti in 1917 – perhaps best known because it is the easiest for schoolchildren to remember, as it is only seven syllables long. It is called *Mattino* (Morning):

> *M'illumino d'immenso*

It means, literally, "I am illumined by the immense." And what does this completely untranslatable work of literature tell us? Absolutely nothing, except to illustrate vividly that what is lost in translation *is* the poetry. As illustrated in the following sample of words, the Italians are certainly expressive and poetic in their untranslatables.

ristretto [ree-*strett*-oh] (noun)

Italy is the country of coffee, and *il ristretto* is the coffee of choice for any self-respecting coffee snob. Stronger than a traditional expresso, a *ristretto* is a double mix of the first, strong half of a traditional expresso pour. It's also the technical term for that tiny little china cup of thick black coffee, set on the counter with a glass of water, that Italians drink standing at the bar, especially on their way to work. The atmosphere is more silent than at any other time of day, because this absurdly small shot of coffee is the Italian starter motor. Following it, the frantic energetic Italy that we know and love bursts into daily life. If you are in Italy just ask for *un caffè* to participate in this ritual.

castrato [kass-*trah*-toh] (noun)

The language of music remains eternally Italian and every musical score tells us so, with its marginal terms of expression and performance. This word, literally, "a eunuch," no longer refers to a physical condition but rather to the quality of a singing voice that for centuries was an integral part of the highest musical tradition in Italy and beyond. Castration allowed the pure sound of a boy's voice to be preserved into adulthood. *Castrati* were still used in the Sistine Chapel choirs in Rome up until 1880 when Pope Leo XIII banned the practice.

attaccabottoni [at-*tac*-ca-*bot*-own-ee] (noun)

This is a bore who "buttonholes" you and tells you long tales of woe. You long to escape from an *attaccabottoni,* but somehow it's always difficult to get away.

magari [mag-*ah*-ree] (noun)

A rich and positive word with multiple uses and sprinkled everywhere in conversation. It is strongly evocative of the ebullient Italian spirit, meaning anything from "even if" to "Rather!" or "You bet!" It has a wonderfully affirmative value, even when expressing no more than a fervent wish such as *Magari fosse vero!* – "If only it were true!"

casomai [*kaz*-oh-mye] (adverb)

An elusive Italian adverb or conjunction meaning anything from "should it be that," "perhaps," or "if" to "just in case" or "in the eventuality." The Italian director Alessandro D'Alatri used the word as a title for his 2002 film about the uncertainties facing a young couple beginning married life.

mettere in piazza [meh-*tear*-er een pee-*aht*-zah] (idiom)

Literally, "to put it out in the town square," this phrase summons a vivid picture of a couple colorfully and loudly airing their most intimate and private secrets in the most public place possible. Such an action captures both the fiery Italian spirit and setting, and the idea collides forcefully with keeping arguments behind closed doors.

Dutch

The Netherlands is home to the usual clichés – windmills, dikes, butter, bicycles, tulips, overboiled vegetables – but, among all these, an eminently practical and sensible people unfairly known elsewhere in Europe as "cheeseheads" because of their high consumption of dairy products. The Dutch language itself is home to a hundred skating expressions that may or may not be metaphors for life, such as *Hij heeft een scheve schaats gereden* "He's been skating on one side," and lots of plainspoken sayings, like *De molen gaat niet om met wind die voorbij is* – "The windmill doesn't care for the wind that's gone past." The following examples show only too clearly that the Dutch have a very particular and often unpronounceable way of going about things.

uitwaaien [*oot*-vay-en] (verb)
A most useful and attractive verb meaning "to walk in the wind for fun." It conjures up a charming image of eighteenth-century Dutch landscape paintings.

de doofpot [der *doof*-pott] (noun)
Literally, "the extinguisher," this is a common Dutch response to any type of scandal that urges everyone to look the other way so that the whole thing is forgotten and dies without a trace. The British demonstrate a similar instinct in their saying "let sleeping dogs lie," but in the Netherlands, *de doofpot* could come across as more of a national consensus policy.

uitbuiken [*oot*-book-en] (verb)

Another "enjoyment" verb like *uitwaaien,* but this time based on the word for stomach, *buik,* meaning "to take your time at dinner, relaxing between courses." A nicely untranslatable extension of this meaning was recently created in a newspaper headline just before Christmas, wishing everyone *Spiritueel Uitbuiken* – literally "spiritual expansiveness of stomach." It summed up that real Christmas feeling, or *gezelligheid,* of being together in a feeling of peace and unity between people. With a full stomach, of course.

krentenkakker [*kren*-ten-kak-er] (noun)

Just so we don't mix up our Dutch with our German, this is the same word as the German *Korinthenkacker* ("raisin crapper"), but in Holland it means someone who doesn't like spending money. I'm afraid the equivalent to the German *Korinthenkacker* is expressed somewhat more graphically in Dutch as *mierenneuker* – "ant f--ker."

gezellig [*chayz*-ell-ich] (adjective)

This word is reportedly found a dozen times a day on Dutch lips. In its essence perhaps it just means anything "typically Dutch," which by extension means anything good, from "having a fun time" to "cozy" to "homely." Eating *oliebollen,* which are fried dough balls with raisins, on New Year's Eve is apparently very *gezellig.* Beyond that it is hard to get a Dutch person to be more precise!

onderbuik [*on*-der-book] (noun)

This word literally translates as the "underbelly" and from this sense we also get *de onderbuik van de samenleving* – "the lowest" or even "criminal classes of society." But it seems only Dutch people get *onderbuikgevoelens,* which evokes these connotations to translate as "underbelly feelings." This word is mainly used to express politically incorrect or socially unacceptable sentiments. Dutch politicians have sometimes been accused of appealing to *onderbuikgevoelens* on the issue of immigration, for instance.

Spanish

L ooking at modern Spanish, we still find the huge influence of the Arabic language, dating from the centuries of Islamic occupation. We also have to take into account the regional dialects and languages of Gallego, Catalan, Basque, not to mention *caló* (gypsy), while the enormous variety of Latin American local terms from Chile to Mexico is a study in itself. How do we translate the simple word *chango* when the *Dictionary of the Real Academia* tells us that it has some eight different meanings, from "elegant man" to "shopping trolley," depending on where you are in the continent?

San Francisco radio journalist Rose del Castillo Guilbault, reveals that sometimes translation and the adoption of words results in an unhappy corruption of meaning. She describes the meaning of "macho" for herself, coming from a Mexican background, in contrast with the image of this word in American culture.

"What is macho?" That depends on which side of the border you come from. Although it's not unusual for words and expressions to lose their subtlety in translation, the negative connotations of "macho" in the United States are troublesome to Hispanics. *"Es muy macho,"* the women in my family [in Mexico] nod approvingly, describing a man they respect. But in the United States, when women say, "He's so macho," it's with disdain. The Hispanic *macho* is manly, responsible, hardworking, a man in charge, a patriarch. A man who expresses strength through silence. What the Yiddish language would call a *mensch*. The American "macho" is a

chauvinist, a brute, uncouth, selfish, loud, abrasive, capable of inflicting pain, and sexually promiscuous. Quintessential "macho" models in America are Sylvester Stallone, Arnold Schwarzenegger, and Charles Bronson. In their movies, they exude toughness, independence, masculinity. But a closer look reveals their "machismo" is really violence masquerading as courage, sullenness disguised as silence, and irresponsibility camouflaged as independence. If the Hispanic ideal of *macho* were translated to American screen roles, they might be Jimmy Stewart, Sean Connery, and Laurence Olivier.

Spanish has also given us the untranslatable world of Latin American dance – not just "dancing" as we know it, but dance where everything hangs out in the abandonment to rhythm and music. *Flamenco* is forever *flamenco,* but the recent popularity of *salsa, samba, rumba, mambo, cha-cha,* and *marengue* illustrates the intensity of our search for the antidote to Freudian inhibitions. Who needs analysis if you can salsa the night away without falling over? Most of these dances have no equivalent in other tongues, and some, like the intense *tango,* are more than mere dances, but cultural zones in their own right, infused with their own narratives, vocabulary, mood, color, and following.

Here are a few terms that capture something of the untranslatable vitality, variety, and wonder of Spanish culture.

duende [*dwen*-day] (adjective)

This wonderful word captures an entire world of passion, energy, and artistic excellence and describes a climactic show of spirit in a performance or work of art. *Duende* originally meant "imp" or "goblin" and came to mean anything magical. It now has a depth and complexity of meaning that crosses artistic borders, from flamenco dancing to bullfighting. The Spanish poet García Lorca wrote an eloquent essay on *duende* that explores the complex and inspirational flavor of its sense, and I know no better introduction.

aquelarre [ak-ell-*arr*-ay] (noun)

A Spanish borrowing from Basque, a tongue that is itself a linguistic puzzle, bearing absolutely no relation to other European languages. The original Basque word *akelarre* means "the meadow of the male goat," and the word refers to a nighttime gathering of a coven of witches, in a suitably rustic area, to invoke the presence of the devil, who normally participates as a male goat. Well, he would, wouldn't he!

cutre [*koo*-tray] (adjective)

This expressive adjective describes anything that is not to your taste, everything from a bar, a street, a hotel, clothing, to furniture. However, the word expresses not just bad taste or over-the-top taste (the Spanish also use the word *kitsch*) but anything foreign to your own liking or standards. "Tacky" might be the closest English slang gets to this word, but even this misses the disdain with which a Spanish girl might say of her boyfriend, *¡Qué regalo más cutre me dió!*

chungo [*tchun*-goh] (adjective)

From the gypsy word for "ugly" and meaning generally "pretty bad." No translation can get across this word's almost comic sense of disaster. Here's a Spanish joke that illustrates the difference between *bueno, malo,* and *chungo* ("good," "bad," and "*chungo*") through a number of life situations:

Bueno: Your wife is pregnant.
Malo: It's triplets.
Chungo: You had a vasectomy two years ago.

Bueno: Your wife hardly speaks.
Malo: She wants a divorce.
Chungo: She's a lawyer.

paseo [*pass-ay*-oh] (noun)

The time of evening when the heat of the sun is diminishing and the *siesta* is over is the moment of the *paseo*. It is the time when the Spanish dress themselves and their children up to the nines and go out to walk around the main square, or up and down the shade of avenues. It's a time of meeting and looking, seeing and being seen. Late on summer nights, after the *cena,* the same gentle ambling takes place until well after midnight, with small children often, by that time, dozing on their parent's shoulders.

gilipollas [chee-lee-*poll-yass*] (adjective)

This is another word of gypsy origin, that at its root means "innocent" in the sense of "born yesterday." It has become a rich-sounding insult for anyone behaving stupidly and irresponsibly, from bad drivers to thoughtless youth in the streets. *¡Qué gilipollas!*

mañana [mann-*yah*-nah] (noun)

We translate this common word into English as "tomorrow," the day that follows today, but there is a strong possibility that in most parts of the Spanish-speaking world, *mañana* refers to some other indefinite and untranslatable time concept related to the future. It compares well with the Arabic word *bukra.*

pícaro [*pee*-ka-roh] (noun, adjective)

This word has wide and colorful associations. Students of Spanish literature come across *la picaresca* as a style of novel, a kind of episodic storywriting usually involving criminals drifting through society, well-illustrated by Cervantes's *Don Quijote.* The typical *pícaro* is one who lives off his wits in order to survive. *La picaresca* summons up a whole tapestry of human life at its most inventive, ingenious, and resilient. *Pícaro* can mean smart, astute, clever, cunning, mischievous, naughty, shameless, wicked, saucy, impudent, lustful, roguish, dishonorable, bold, daring, racy, brazen, or cheeky. It practically sums up the human condition!

Portuguese

T he Portuguese people are renowned for their warmth and friendliness, so it would be unkind to repeat the impression that speaking Portuguese is just like speaking Spanish but with your mouth full of toffee. But when did any of us last have to speak Portuguese? Like the Greeks, the Portuguese have had to learn other languages to communicate with the outside world, beyond their old colonies, of course. However, a friend of mine who for sheer love studied the language for years was finally vindicated when we were once lost in Beirut and the only person around to tell us the way turned out to be a Portuguese speaker without a word of English.

The Portuguese, among the greatest sailors and explorers of the sixteenth century, left magnificent traces of their culture all over the world, from the depths of the South American rainforest, to the islands and coasts of the China Sea. From Manaus to Macao, their colonial style was one of elegance and grandeur. And regardless of what you may think of the global importance of Portuguese culture, it must be said that it takes a certain self-confidence to build an opera house halfway up the Amazon!

saudade [sow-dah-*day*] (noun)

A kind of intense nostalgia that only Portuguese people are supposed to understand. In Katherine Vaz's definition, which she uses to explain the title of her novel *Saudade,* it is a "yearning so intense for those who are missing, or for vanished times or places, that absence is the most profound presence in one's life. A state of being, rather than merely a sentiment." In his 1912 book on Portugal, literary specialist and translator A. F. G. Bell writes:

The famous *saudade* of the Portuguese is a vague and constant desire for something that does not and probably cannot exist, for something other than the present, a turning towards the past or towards the future; not an active discontent or poignant sadness but an indolent dreaming wistfulness.

fado [*fah*-doh] (noun)

Portuguese song is full of *saudade*, and none more so than the tradition known as *fado* – a culture not just of song but of a deep and sad romanticism that wells up from the soul. The songwriter and poet Nick Cave has commented that we all experience the Portuguese feeling of *saudade*. He sees this intense yearning as the breeding ground for the *fado* love song tradition.

se virar [say vee-*rahr*] (verb)

From Brazilian Portuguese, this literally means "to empty" but is used to describe when you try to do something but you don't have enough knowledge to complete the task.

fora do pinico, mijar [*foh*-rah doh pin-*ee*-coh, mee-*jahr*] (idiom)

Brazilian Portuguese is colorful in its *giria* or slang. The late Carlos Lacerda, a journalist and former governor, noted that, "Brazil is the only country in the world where practically every word is a cussword – even mother." Literally meaning "to pee outside the pisspot," in English this means "to miss the target," or "to say the wrong thing."

Chapter 2

Eastern European Languages

 olik jazyku znas, tolikrat jsi clovekem. This wonderful Czech proverb, impossible to translate exactly, proclaims that you live a new life for every new language you speak. If you know only one language, you live only once.

It is plain, especially in recent history, that eastern European people have had an awful lot to cope with, and all have found their ways of dealing with it. These races are vividly alive, incapable of being lackluster about anything, and their various languages are correspondingly full of vigor and color. In Slovak, you don't just "perspire freely," you "sweat like a donkey in a suitcase." A Hungarian, by his own definition, is someone who enters a swinging door behind you and comes out in front of you. And as for the Czechs, well, their iconoclastic sense of humor is justly famed. Poland is renowned for *zalatwic,* its way of getting around officialdom by going through "someone you know." Modern Russian is said to have numerous untranslatable euphemisms for shirking work, a legacy of seventy years of dispiriting Communist rule.

Most of these eastern European cultures are related through their Slavic inheritance. Hungarian stands out linguistically and is closer to Finnish than to the tongues of its Slavic neighbors. The Serbian author Dragan Velikic̆ writes of the confusing impact that his first experiences of the Hungarian language had on him:

> I have a large collection of Hungarian words in my head, a collection that is both full and empty at the same time.

Full, because I remember the words, I can repeat them, they exist, they exist even for me, as mine – a kind of souvenir of the past from a life I am only now starting anew.

Empty, because I do not know what all these words mean. I remember the words the way one remembers one's own name . . . For instance: *Pillangó utca.* I translated that name to myself as "Pillangó Street," in other words, I did not translate it at all, convinced that it was a name, a street bearing somebody's name. I walked through Budapest as if I had just arrived in Babylon where, by the grace of a god who had yet to become angry or disappointed, everything had a personal name, untranslatable, and thus immediately understandable. Nothing about that feeling changed even when my friend explained to me smilingly that *pillangó* means "butterfly." You are talking about the street of butterflies, she said, about Butterfly Street. But the word *pillangó* was ever after engraved in my mind as the name of a butterfly. There was a "Pillangó butterfly" and it lived in Budapest.

There is a nice echo in this story of how we all learn languages in our childhood. We hear a spoken sound, a noise, and make an association, and even when as adults we may see it is wrong, we never quite lose that "meaning" that we once created for the noise. Here are some untranslatable words from a rich and varied region of the European continent.

Czech and Hungarian

I t is generally understood that you can only be a true Czech if you speak the language. It is plain that they are very proud of their tongue and this is clearly illustrated in the Czech word for a German speaker. The word is *ne'mci,* which derives from the word for "mutes." According to a Czech, if you don't speak the language you don't have anything worth saying. The Czech language is also famous for its consonants and you can find as many as five in a row, such as in the word for "ice-cream," *zmrzlina.* Try saying this well-known tongue twister that does entirely without vowels – *strc˘ prst skrz krk* – which means "stick your finger through your neck."

The Hungarian language, on the other hand, doesn't have many relatives in Europe at all and is most similar to Finnish and Turkish. A language with a lot of words that mean the same thing, Hungarian has two hundred different words describing the breed and the coloring of a horse.

litost (Czech) [*lee*-tosht] (noun)

This is an untranslatable emotion that only a Czech person would suffer from, defined by Milan Kundera as "a state of torment created by the sudden sight of one's own misery." Devices for coping with extreme stress, suffering, and change are often special and unique to cultures and born out of the meeting of despair with a keen sense of survival.

vodník (Czech) [*vod*-neek] (noun)

These sinister creatures are malevolent water spirits from Slavonic folklore that come into being whenever a child is drowned. Resembling a man with webbed feet and green hair, *vodníks* drown unwary swimmers and then imprison the souls of their victims in jars, trapping them forever in the underwater kingdom.

pohoda (Czech) [*poh*-hoh-dah] (noun)
As if to compensate for the dreadful emotion of *litost,* only Czechs can enjoy the blissful state known as *pohoda.* The saying goes *Jsem v pohodi* and translates as "I'm in pohoda." So what exactly is *pohoda?* It's hard to say, except that it's a pain-free, trouble-free state that we should all like to share in.

egyem meg a szivedet (Hungarian) [egd-yem-meg-a-siv-ver-det] (idiom)
This literally translates as "I'd like to eat your heart" and rather than being a grisly, bloodthirsty kind of expression it is one said with great affection. It is usually to a small child who has done something so nice or good that it has emotionally touched an adult's heart.

egyszer volt budán kutyavásár (Hungarian) [egd-zair volt bood-an koocha-vah-sha] (idiom)
An enigmatic Hungarian idiom that literally translates as "there was a dog-market in Buda only once." The meaning in English is close to "a favorable opportunity that only happens once." It is something to be grasped with two hands, otherwise you will find yourself regretting it at a later date.

Polish

D iminutive forms in Polish add a certain charm, emotion, and atmosphere that cannot be carried directly across in translation. Diminutives are used to indicate that something is physically small or little, and often they carry an affectionate form when they are referring to normal objects. These types of words lie at the heart of the cultural divide, and it is often very easy to convey the wrong impression, trapped by this quirk of language.

You can say "cat" in Polish in at least five ways – *kot, kotek, koteczek, kotulek, kotuleczek*. Each word means something quite different, and the meanings vary from a reference to your relationship with the cat in question to describing its size.

The words for "milk" are more straightforward, *mleko* translating as "milk," *mleczko* as "small milk." However, the Polish words for smile *us'miech*, "a smile," and *us'mieszek*, "a little smile," have more of an ironic twist.

narobic' bigosu [na-*ro*-beetch bee-*go*-soo] (idiom)

The expression *narobic' bigosu* means "to make a mess" or cause problems or confusion. It comes from the noun *bigos*, which is a popular Polish dish made with sauerkraut, sausage, and mushrooms as the basic ingredients. You then add whatever else you have in the cupboard to the stew. Just so we are clear, if you are setting out to tell someone you're making *bigos* for supper, this is expressed as *zrobic' bigos*.

nie dla wszystkich skrzypce graja [ni-*e* dla *vshist*-keech *skship*-ze gra yonh] (proverb)

This Polish proverb translates literally into English as "the violin doesn't play for everybody." The Polish word for violin is *skrzypce* and this word derives from the word *skrzyp*, which means "creak" or "groan." While there is no common translation or equivalent in English, we all know the horrible ear-splitting screeching and scratchiness of a violin in the hands of a novice. Next time you see a person attempting a task for which they quite obviously lack the required skill you could obliquely drop an observation that "the violin doesn't play for everybody."

baba [_bah_-bah] (noun)

This word has a number of meanings. Differing from the direct equivalent of "woman" in Polish, which is the word _kobieta_, most often _baba_ is a derogatory word for a woman. It can be translated in various ways to mean "stupid woman," to comment on the appearance of or sexually objectify the woman it describes, or in a way that incredulously implies admiration – "she is wise but she is a woman." However, _baba_ is also one of the first words a baby learns. When spoken by a baby it means "grandma," so most grandmas love to hear this word from their one-year-old grandchildren.

pokazac´ komus´ gdzie raki zimuja [po-_ka_-zatch _ko_-moosh gdje _ra_-kee zee-_moo_-yonh] (proverb)

This wonderfully visual proverb literally means "to show someone where crayfish winter" (as in where they spend the winter.) But it is used as an example of teaching someone a lesson, or extracting a revenge. Perhaps the American slang to "sleep with the fishes" comes closest to the flavor of this expression.

hart ducha [hahrt _doo_-hah] (noun)

We are back in the world of the Spanish _machismo_ and the Yiddish _mensch_ for _hart ducha_. It literally means "strength of spirit," or "strength of will." A man needs to be a man, and this word covers the mental self-discipline that it requires. But, more than this, it describes a man who is physically brave and will not cower, yield to, or flee from danger, attacks on his person, or oppression of his spirit. This noun literally translates as "strength of spirit" or "strength of will." Polish people are renowned for their independent character and, given the nature of Polish history, _hart ducha_ has been witnessed many times in the character of the Polish people.

Russian

T ranslating from Russian is considered by some to be impossible, such is the particular quality of the Russian way of seeing the world. Conditioned by this feeling, perhaps, the well-known Russian translator Vladimir Muravyov, interviewed in *The Russian Journal* in July 2001, went so far as to say:

> Actually, all writings are untranslatable. If anyone thinks that he or she knows English or other languages and is able to translate, it's just rubbish. It is only by some mystic coincidences that a felicitous translation can appear.

Vladimir Nabokov also came up against a great amount of criticism, particularly over his controversial translation of the Russian soul epic by Aleksandr Pushkin, *Eugene Onegin*. In reply to those who questioned his literal, rather than poetic, translation of the great work, he is reputed to have said, "It's impossible to convey the original, so learn Russian!"

We must remember that Russia, like its fellow Slavic nations, is a country whose culture is going through rapid change. Stephen Ryan of Eichi University, attending an English teaching conference in Khabarovsk, Russia, reports on cross-cultural issues and the ensuing problems for translators and interpreters:

> There was particular emphasis on words in Russian and English which seem to be untranslatable. "Demonstration" was offered as an example. Apparently it is an old saw that Americans demonstrate against things and Russians in favour of things, so the word has quite different connotations in English and Russian. A member of the audience pointed out that this is no longer

true, that increasingly Russians are holding demonstrations against the government. This pattern repeated itself many times: claims about differences between Russian and English were moderated by remarks on the changing connotations of Russian words. The Russian language, it seems, is keeping pace with the rapid changes in Russian society as a whole, leaving translators gasping to keep up.

Notwithstanding these changes in Russian society, perhaps because of its long experience with authoritarian politics and grace-and-favor rule, we find some deeply entrenched characteristics. For instance, levels and qualities of human relationships are richly developed, even in comparison with other Slavic tongues. This wealth of words for different kinds of relationships (in addition to kin) provides evidence of Russian culture's interest in the area of human dealings with one another.

Roughly speaking, relations are categorized by their "closeness" or "strength," perhaps also hinting at their trustworthiness. *Drug* is someone extremely close to us, much more so than the English word "friend." *Podruga,* "female friend," refers to a bond less powerful than *drug* but still stronger than "friend," closer to "girlfriend" or "lover." *Prijatel'* or *prijatel'nica* is rather more distant and *znakomyj* is still more distant, although closer than the supposed English equivalent word, "acquaintance."

On another level the Russian character has an intensely spiritual side. The quest for *istina*, meaning "higher values," is never far from the surface of the Russian culture. There is a range of value-laden, untranslatable Russian attitudes, such as *podlec,* "base person who inspires contempt," *marzavec,* "base person who inspires disgust," and *negogjaj,* "base person who inspires indignation." It is the idealization of certain *istina* attitudes and the corresponding contempt for others that provides the Russian self-image with an edge over that of other races.

poshlost [*puhsh*-lust] (noun)

This word, which one can imagine uttered with a contemptuous curl of the lip, indicates an acute awareness of the hollowness of false values and the need to deride and deflate them. The Russian writer Vladimir Nabokov devoted many pages to a damning commentary on *poshlost,* which he claimed to have fought against all his life. He describes *poshlost* as "cheap, sham, common, pink–and–blue, high falutin', in bad taste." Russian dictionaries also offer fairly negative definitions such as "spiritually and morally base, petty, worthless, mediocre" and "commonplace, spiritually and morally base, devoid of higher interests and needs."

dusa [doo-*shah*] (noun)

Simply, this translates as "soul," but *dusa* is much more than this. It is seen as a person's spiritual, moral, and emotional core. It is an internal theater where a person's moral and emotional life is staged.

razbliuto [ros-blee-*oo*-toe] (noun)

This melancholic, bittersweet word is used to describe lost love. Specifically, it's a feeling a person has for someone he or she once loved but no longer feels the same way about. It's a brilliantly succinct word and captures that feeling of the maddeningly ephemeral nature of love.

osuzhdat [ah-sooj-*daht*] (verb)

The tendency to *osuzhdat,* that is, to "roughly condemn" other people in conversation, to make absolute moral judgments, and to link moral judgments with emotions, is reflected in a wide variety of Russian words and phrases. This is linked with the cultural emphasis on "absolute truth" and "higher values" in general.

rodnye [rohd-*nee*-eh] (noun)

The concept of *rodnye* is usually translated into English with the word "relatives," but this word does not really even approximate the meaning. *Rodnye* usually refers to the immediate family, to close relatives rather than distant ones. It is also extended to close people outside the family. From a Russian perspective, *rodnye* are beloved and indispensable. The word reflects the value of close family ties in Russian culture and also shows that the boundary between kin and non-kin can be blurred. What is really essential is the existence of unconditional emotional ties, and these ties are seen as an important part of one's identity.

tovarisch [ta-*vahr*-ish] (noun)

Usually translated as "comrade," the word *tovarisch* is infused with political meaning and was of central importance in the Soviet era. Being addressed as *tovarisch* was a sign of belonging. Losing this title or the right to use it toward others was a sign of exclusion and a possible prelude to arrest or imprisonment. If a single word could be cited as the key to the workings of Soviet society, it would probably have to be *tovarisch*.

svoboda [sva-*boh*-dah] (noun)

At first glance the Russian concept of *svoboda* seems very similar to the English word "freedom." But it can also be used in a slightly different sense to mean something like "ease and relaxation." The concept of *svoboda* suggests the image of a child unwrapped from his swaddling clothes and feeling pleasure and relief at being able to move his arms and legs without any restriction. Similarly, *svoboda* suggests a feeling of well-being, caused by the absence of pressure or constraining bonds.

yolki-palki [*yohl*-kee-*pahl*-kee] (idiom)

A peculiar Russian expression that could express surprise, dismay, or pleasure, depending on the situation. The phrase literally translates as "fir trees and sticks" but is probably approximated in English by the expression "holy cow!"

~ Chapter 3 ~

Yiddish Language

Y iddish is rediscovering itself as a rich cultural phenomenon and a serious object of study, despite its linguistic complexity and its perception as a corrupt language. Around three million people speak Yiddish as their first language worldwide, while around six million people speak Hebrew. Hebrew is considered the "language of sanctity" among the Jewish languages but today modern Hebrew is a fusion language, with Yiddish as its bedrock.

Yiddish was spoken by millions of Jews at its height, it was the principal tongue of the Ashkenazi Jews. Jewish historian, David Shyovitz, writes that it was born out of "a modified version of medieval German that included elements of Laaz, biblical and Mishnaic Hebrew, and Aramaic [that] came to be the primary language of Western European Jews" from the tenth century onward. By the seventeenth century, Yiddish had become a written as well as a spoken language using Hebrew script.

The Holocaust struck at the very heart of the Yiddish language. A huge number of the surviving speakers were killed in the Second World War. Despite such obstacles, Shyovitz writes:

> Yiddish is today enjoying a resurgence. Several populations use it as their main language: primarily the generation that lived during and immediately after the Holocaust and the ultra-Orthodox populations living in New York and parts of Israel.

Yiddish delivers a rich and wonderful harvest of terms, ideas, and descriptions. A surprising number of words have found their way into English, including words that we have perhaps come to take for granted such as *boo-boo, glitch, gelt, bagel,* and *mensch.* Here is a selection of the more delightfully untranslatable ones.

chutzpah [*hoots*-pah] (noun)

This word roughly translates as a kind of presumption layered with arrogance, although that would deny the underlying humor of the term. You can't say this word without appreciating its gutsiness. It is audacity without shame and, provided the mix is more spunk than impudence, not necessarily an undesirable quality. To wheel out the old cliché, *chutzpah* is best summed up by the boy who kills his parents and then pleads for mercy from the judge – on grounds that he's an orphan.

schmuck [*shmuk*] (noun)

From the German for "ornament," this is a surprisingly innocent derivation, considering that it has come to mean "penis." Not a word to be uttered lightly, and certainly not in polite company. However, used discerningly in the right circumstance, it has considerable force as an insult.

l'havdil [*lav*-deel] (idiom)

This word derives from the Hebrew "to separate." Meaning something approximating "forgive the comparison," *l'havdil* is a helpful speech device that allows the user to boast while appearing decently modest.

megillah [may-*gill*-ah] (noun)

From the Hebrew word for "scroll," the *megillah,* or the Biblical book of *Esther*, is read on the Jewish festival of Purim. In colloquial speech, it is a versatile term covering anything long, complicated, dull, or unnecessarily dragged out. "Don't give me a *megillah*" means "spare me the details." In recent years, it's also come to mean a major event or cause for excitement.

bupkis [*bup*-kiss] (noun)

This word, literally meaning "beans," has come to mean "nothing" or something that is worthless. It is generally spoken in disgust or despair, and "I haven't got *bubkis*" relates to the English phrase "I haven't got a bean."

kvell [*kvell*] (verb)

From the German *quellen,* meaning "to gush" or "swell." When a person *kvells*, they seem to beam with irrepressible pride and pleasure. Nothing makes many Jewish people *kvell* so much as the achievements of their children or grandchildren.

schlock [*shlok*] (noun, adjective)

This word originally derived from the German word for "hit" or "blow." *Shlock* at first came to refer to damaged merchandise and then to merchandise of inferior quality. If you get trash, ask if it came from the "schlock house."

schmooze [*shmooz*] (verb)

Whereas "networking" is aimed unambiguously at self-promotion, and doubtless you can go on a course to learn it, *schmoozing* denotes a more warmly human activity. A good *schmooze* is when you connect with others in a meaningful and authentic way, perhaps when you least expect it. Unusual for a Yiddish untranslatable, it's used widely in British as well as North American speech.

nudnik [*nood*-nik] (noun)

From the Russian word *nudnyi* meaning "tedious," a *nudnik* is a pestering or irritating person. It has now been creatively extended to form the word *phudnik,* cleverly translating as a pest with a PhD.

kvetchtz [ke-*ve*-tch] (noun)

A *kvetchtz* is the deepest of sighs for all the burdens and troubles of the entire world, past, present, and future. An unhappy person sighing is a *kvetchtzer.*

tachlis [*tah*-kles] (noun)

When people talk *tachlis*, they get down to the nitty-gritty. *Tachlis* is the bottom line, the fine detail. Originating from the Hebrew word for "purpose" or "end," the term can be applied to the way one feels about something as well as to the specifics of something. Once the tachlis of a deal have been sorted, the salesman might then say "*Taches offen tisch*." Literally, "ass on the table," this means it's time to close the deal. Outside of business, the best equivalent is "step up to the plate."

luftmensch [*looft*-mensh] (noun)

Literally this translates as "one who lives on air." You can get the idea. There is usually one of these in every family – an impractical person who is overly dependent on the family for survival.

nakhes [noch-ess] (plural noun)

This word is not quite accurately translated as "the joys of parenthood" and is generally spoken with an ironic turn of phrase. From the Hebrew word *nahat* meaning "contentment," *nakhes* are truly and genuinely all the pleasures that parents get from their children!

chazerai [*tchah*-zuh-rye] (noun)

This word literally translates as "pig's feed." It has come to be the Yiddish word that refers to what we call in English eating "junk food," pizza, sweets, and chips, all in one sitting. However, *chazerai* is not limited to describing food. The word can also be used to describe household or other kinds of junk.

mishigas [*mih*-shi-*goss*] (noun)

This is a very useful Yiddish word and has been fully adopted into contemporary U. S. English. It describes a craziness, nonsense, or something unbelievably stupid that someone (usually a politician) has done. More affectionately, it can describe a friend or relative's personal eccentricities.

Chapter 4

Nordic Languages

Nordic people are not like any other people in the world. Thomas Hylland Eriksen writes, "Foreign stereotypes tend to depict Scandinavians as wealthy, enlightened, rational and bored Protestants with strong welfare states, lax rules of sexual morality and an institutionalised yearning for nature and simplicity." But there are significant differences, for those who can see them, between the nationalities. Eriksen quotes the following example:

> A Swede, a Dane and a Norwegian are shipwrecked on the proverbial desert island. A genie appears out of thin air, informing them that they can each have a wish granted. The Swede immediately says, "I want to go home to my large and comfortable bungalow with the Volvo, video and slick IKEA furniture." So he vanishes. The Dane then says, "I want to go back to my cozy little flat in Copenhagen, to sit on my soft sofa, feet on the table, next to my sexy girlfriend, with a six-pack of lagers." Off he flies. The Norwegian, after giving the problem a bit of thought, then tells the genie, "Cor, I suddenly feel so terribly lonely here, so I guess I wish for my two friends to come back."

Denmark, of course, is where both Swedes and Norwegians go to enjoy themselves in the land of *hygge. The Copenhagen Post* reported, "No single aspect of Danish culture has baffled foreigners more. A near-untranslatable concept incorporating elements of English coziness, Norwegian *koselighet,* Finnish *vilhtylisyys,* French *douillet,* Dutch *gezelligheid* and Irish crack." Ah, that's clear now. And what exactly might *hyggekrog (hygge*-nooks) be? Here we have to turn to some serious academic research, and

Professor Judith Friedman Hansen has written just the study we need, *The Proxemics of Danish Daily Life*. She tells us, "familiarity is the key element, a closed-in state of stable predictableness associated with small-scale gatherings of people." This means creating a *hyggekrog* – a protective space characterized by low tables under a subdued light, with candles, flowers, food, and drink. Only certain folk will ever be invited into this space. Hansen adds, "one would not ordinarily speak of *hygge* with strangers or even acquaintances, it is a state most often linked with one's circle of close friends and family."

By the very nature of *hygge* it follows that the Swedes and Norwegians never get invited. To the Danish, the nearest foreigners can get is *råhygge* – "raw" *hygge,* a rough-edged version, and a mere copy of it.

The Finns, despite having an almost totally Arctic climate, have made a virtue of their perpetual cold by insulating themselves in saunas, and enjoy a custom known as *löyly,* that incredible heat wave that engulfs you when you throw water on the hot stove. Not only this, but they then go outside to beat themselves with *vihta* (or *vasta,* depending on what part of the country you live in), a leafy bundle of birch to slap against the body in order to go back inside and increase the *löyly* sensation. All very purifying and healthy for a nation whose language enjoys a surfeit of vowels.

What then unites these nations and cultures? *Folkelighed* or *folklighet,* depending on where you are, is a central concept throughout the fundamentally antiélitist Scandinavian culture. United, but in friendly tension, the Nordic countries represent a wonderland of untranslatable customs, beliefs, and nuances of social behavior.

Danish

The Danes themselves will be among the first to say of their speech, *det er inget sprak, det er en halsinfektion* – "it's no language, it's a throat infection!"

Nordic languages are quite similar and often speakers of one can generally understand speakers of another. However, there are real risks of occasional misunderstandings because there are a good few words that look the same but have different meanings in the different languages. A Dane may run into trouble when speaking about *rolig* to a Swede. Meaning "calm," "tranquil," and "restful" in Danish, this identical word means "funny," "amusing," and "entertaining" in Swedish. So when you're told that a certain restaurant is *rolig,* it's good to be entirely sure which language you are hearing!

janteloven [*yann*-te-loh-wen] (noun)

This exists outside Denmark but is rarely described so succinctly. It is sometimes translated as "the tall poppy syndrome" – you may put yourself on a pedestal but be prepared to get knocked off. It is the Law of Jante, as elaborated in a novel by Aksel Sandemose. So you may be good, but you're no better than the rest of us. We're all equal and all equally good. Who the *hell* do you think you are?!

smørrebrød [*smerr*-er-brerd] (noun)

The world–famous Danish open sandwich. But isn't an open sandwich not just a closed one that has been ceremonially prized open like a reluctant clam or a mummy's tomb? No indeed, for to cover the top of an open sandwich would be to abuse the filling, or rather the topping. It would deface the trimmings and humiliate the emancipated pink prawns that grace it, lying there in all their naked glory, parading themselves and basking amid a shallow sea of fresh watercress, luring potential diners to sample their wares. We should

beware of contaminating this concept by association with the common and rather plain sandwich of middle–class picnics.

festlig [*fest*-lee] (adjective)

Festlig is an adjective formed from the noun *fest,* meaning "party," and any public festivities in general. The adjective, however, is far more versatile, and is used about things as diverse as wallpaper, table decorations, clothing, an evening with friends, people who are the life and soul of the party, and of course, the ubiquitous Danish parties themselves. It can also refer to someone who's a live wire, a good laugh, full of party spirit, and generally has a festive outlook on everything.

folkelig [*foll*-ke-lee] (noun)

Folk means "people" in general but "a people" specifically. What of *folkelig?* Belonging, related, and pertaining to the people? Popular? Let's look at some examples. *Folkelig idræt* is popular sport, not of international standing but firmly rooted in women pounding the pavement in sweatpants. *Folkelig oplysning* is everything from public information to popular enlightenment. Harking back to the common Nordic trait *folkelighed, folkelig* is indicative of a culture where elitism is unacceptable and popular culture has always had an eminent position.

Swedish

I n spoken form, Swedish is by far the easiest of the Nordic languages to follow. Several words in Swedish sound the same as in English but have different meanings. For example *kokt* in Swedish is pronounced "cooked," but specifically means "boiled." When your Swedish waiter asks if you would like your breakfast egg "cooked," he will be confused if you answer, "Yes please, fried." Even more problematic is the Swedish word *gå*. It is pronounced "go," but it does not mean "go." Literally translated, it means "walk."

skål [*skohl*] (noun)

The Swedish have certain rules about drinking *snaps*, their national drink. You may not drink *snaps* whenever you want to at the dinner table. When someone wants a drink, they propose a *skål,* and often it is accompanied by a song:

Helan går, sjung hoppfallerallan lallan la.
Helan går, sjung hoppfallerallanlej.
Och den som inte helan tar,
han inte heller halvan får.
Helan går – sjung hoppfallerallanlej!

Att ta helan means "taking the first *snaps*." The first glass is known as *helan* and the second *snaps* is known as *halvan.* In the last line of the song, you take a short pause and traditionally drain your glass. These days it is acceptable just to take a sip, however. These rousing words in the song encourage you to start drinking so that you can continue drinking. And you can continue drinking! After *helan* and *halvan* come the third glass, *tersen,* the fourth glass, *kvarten,* the fifth glass, *kvinten,* and if you still want another glass, the last one is called *lille manasse.*

lagom [lag-*ohm*] (adverb, adjective, noun)

The Swedish culture could be summarized in the word *lagom*. It refers to an undefined state between extremes, such as "not too much, not too little," or "just right." It can refer to the temperature of a warm bath, or the correct fit of a jacket. But these translations do not fully capture the true meaning of the word. Swedish commentator Dr. Bengt Gustavsson, argued that the *lagom* mentality can be seen as the trait that gives Swedish society its characteristic stability and yet an openness to external influences. The word alludes subconsciously to the avoidance of both conspicuous success and humiliating failure, which is deeply ingrained in the Swedish psyche. It is the inclination among Swedes to shun ostentation, accept modest rewards, be good team players – to fly beneath the radar.

bejakela [bay-*ah*-kah] (noun)

A word that frequently recurs in Swedish and is quite untranslatable outside the Scandinavian and Germanic languages, it encapsulates a whole philosophy. *Livsbejakelse* consists of *liv,* meaning "life," and *bejakelse,* meaning "saying yes," hence, "affirmation of life." *Bejaka* means enthusiastic, optimistic, or joyful attitude, and, when applied to life, signifies far more than just agreeing to live. Within this one word we sense a greeting – a welcome to all the vicissitudes that life may bring and an understanding acceptance of people and things as they are.

allemansrätt [*al*-er-manss-rett] (noun)

This is the name of a law in Sweden, literally, "everyone's right," which enables anyone to move around freely amid nature and gather things in publicly designated areas that are capable of growing back, such as mushrooms, fruit, berries, and flowers. Many Swedes take advantage of this legislatively enshrined freedom to collect all sorts of comestibles, as you will see during the height of the respective mushroom, berry, fruit, and nut seasons!

Norwegian

Everything about Norway, a country that finally won its independence only in 1905, is a welcome and delightful mix of old and new. It's a country where human beings sit comfortably within beautiful and unspoiled nature – *miljø,* Norwegian for "society," also means "environment" – where nearly every building merges with the forest and rocky shorelines, and everyone has a boat along with a remote *hytte,* complete with logs and skis stored beside it. For a race whose past is one of daring sagas told for centuries in an oral tradition, it is also noteworthy that the Norwegian word for "history" and "story" is the same, *historie.* Here are some quintessentially untranslatable Norwegian ways of doing things – past, present, and future.

nidstang [*nid*-stang] (noun)
A runic cursing pole used by the Vikings as a way of bringing destruction and disturbance to their enemies. These long poles were carved with insults and curses and ceremonies were performed to activate their destructive magic. The pole was intended to disrupt and anger the *landvaettir,* or "earth spirits," living in the ground beneath the enemy's house. Believe it or not, there are those even today who continue this tradition.

seter [*say*-ter] (noun)
The *seter* was the high and remote "summer farm" where cattle and sheep were taken for the summer pastures – a custom that still survives today in parts of Europe. A shepherd or milkmaid

would stay with the animals all summer, living in a small hut, making butter and cheese that was regularly taken down to sell at market. *Seter* huts were often built together, creating small communities that made their own entertainment during those summer weeks. As people left the land, the *seter* tradition gradually died away, but these age-old ties have survived and Norwegians make a regular flight from modern comforts to their remote *hytte,* or cabin, in all its primitive simplicity and silence.

kunnskåping [*kuhnss*-shay-ping] (noun)

Norway is not all huts, forests, and line dancing; it is also an innovative, thoughtful, and enterprising nation with a language that can change to keep up with the times. A clever creation of Norwegian is the new concept of *kunnskåping,* a punning combination of the words *kunnskåp,* "knowledge," and *verdiskaping,* "value creation," which has been inventively translated as "knowledging." It is hard to summarize exactly what this means, but in business it centers on the idea of developing "intellectual capital" as a profit-making resource. In education, it centers on the creation of knowledge and meaning that is central to the process of learning. It's a word that you should certainly toss into the ring at your first Norwegian dinner party, just to see what happens.

utepils [*oot*-er-pillss] (noun)

You have to live through the long dark months of a Norwegian winter to appreciate the annual Norwegian rite of *utepils.* Literally it means "the first drink of the year taken out of doors." Easter is barely past, with its tradition of *hyttepåske* – your Easter visit to your remote cabin – and the days are at last getting longer. Although it's still practically freezing, everyone is lining up to invite you to a first *utepils* get-together at their favorite bar.

Finnish

F inland is a Nordic country, but is not part of Scandinavia, and the historical roots of Finnish differ from those of the Scandinavian languages. Finnish is a Fenno–Ugrian language, originating in central Russia and distantly related to Hungarian.

Finnish uses a complex inflection system instead of articles and prepositions, and even a familiar word like *taksi* meaning, of course "taxi," can appear in several forms such as *taksiin*, "into a taxi," *taksissa*, "in a taxi," and *taksilla*, "by taxi."

Rautatieasemakirjakauppa is a fine example of the Finnish habit of joining words without articles or prepositions. It becomes much easier to understand if split up:

Rauta	*tie*	*asema*	*kirja*	*kauppa*
Iron	road	shelter	book	shop

Now we can see the literal translation. Is it any clearer? It means, of course, the "railway station bookshop."

The fact that Finnish works so comfortably without subjects gives the language a Taoist character. It is more concerned with being than doing, and more interested in the action than the actor.

hankikanto [hun-kee-*kun*-toh] (noun)

This is a typical Finnish word that resists translation into many languages. *Hankikanto* is a frozen crust on the surface of snow that is strong enough to walk on. This matters to anyone planning a long winter trek, as snow conditions affect the choice of route and equipment.

aina on oksan ottajia, kun on kuusen kantajia [*eye*-nar on *ok*-sun *ot*-tar-ya *koon* on-*koo*-sen *kun*-tu-ya] (proverb)

A disparaging Finnish proverb that captures a worldwide phenomenon. Roughly translatable as "if there is someone to

carry the fir tree, there will be no shortage of people willing to hold a branch to help," it enigmatically suggests that there will always be many people around to grab the coattails of someone else's success, all too willing to participate in sharing the credit for another person's work.

kalakukko [*kul*-u-*kook*-koh] (noun)

This is a traditional Finnish food that has a mysterious and oddly untranslatable name. Although *kalakukko* literally means "fish rooster," it has nothing to do with poultry. Dictionaries suggest "Finnish fish pasty," but "Finnish fish loaf" gives a better idea. "Rye bread loaf with fish and pork filling" is a reasonable description of this dish.

älä maalaa pirua seinälle [*al*-am-*are*-lar *pi*-rew-are *say*-nal-lay] (proverb)

This Finnish proverb roughly translates as "Don't paint a demon on the wall." It is an exhortation not to spend time worrying with no reason about worst–case scenarios because they most likely will not happen. Alternatively, it is an expression uttered, like the English "jinx" or "knock on wood," when you have superstitious fear of something spoken aloud coming true.

Icelandic

Among the fascinating Nordic cultures, Iceland is perhaps the most remarkable. It is a country where reading its medieval sagas is almost like reading yesterday's newspapers, the language has changed so little over the centuries. If a character from one of these sagas magically appeared on the streets of any town in Iceland, he would have little difficulty finding his way around. The country's beliefs are steeped in medievalism as well, and almost govern the procedural red tape. Until recently, the Ministry of Public Works had a special office for advising on the location of elf-mounds. These mounds were not to be disturbed during the construction of a road or a new building.

Iceland is also unique in boasting a National Heroes Cemetery where all the occupants are poets – not a general or even a foot soldier in sight, as the country has no defense forces of its own. Clearly these are folk who live in a different kind of world from mainland Europe!

There is another peculiar Icelandic tradition that any encounter with the language will reveal. The concept of family names, passed down through generations, was unknown in Iceland until quite recently. The traditional system works like this:

> A man named Sven marries a girl named Gudrun, and they agree that if they have a son he will be called Bertil and if they have a daughter she will be called Anna. If eventually they have both, the son will be known as Bertil Svensson, and the daughter will be known as Anna Gudrunsdottir.

The oddity that this kind of naming system produces? If you look up a telephone directory in Iceland, you will find listings under Christian names. Here are some more delightful Icelandic untranslatables.

saga [*sah*-gah] (noun)

A long story of heroic achievement, especially a medieval prose narrative in Old Norse of Old Icelandic. It has also come to mean a long, involved, rambling, seemingly never-ending account, or tales of incidents. Literally, it means "narrative."

land-nam [*land*-nam] (idiom)

This word was coined by the East Indian scholar Ananda Coomaraswamy. *Land-nam* derives from the Icelandic tradition of claiming ownership of a place through weaving a mythic metaphor of plants, animals, and geography of a place into a unique mythic story. It is the sanctification of new land by mythologizing it.

allthing [*all-thing*] (noun)

Iceland is perhaps the only Western nation to have its official parliament meeting in a field, something that dates back to 930 A.D. When it meets, this august body is known as the *Allthing,* an ancient word with its roots in the Germanic *Ding,* or "judgment." It was the custom at this annual event for a *lövsögmathr* to recite the whole law from memory for the good of the assembly.

álfreka [*ohl*-fray-kah] (noun)

Appreciation of elves in Iceland is a serious business, according to Nigel Pennick, writer on spiritual traditions. One of the very worst Norse curses that can be invoked is the *álfreka*, literally, the "driving away of the elves" or the earth spirits from a place, which leaves the ground spiritually dead.

Chapter 5

Middle Eastern Languages

I t is very clear when the holy book of a certain area is alternatively known as "The Untranslatable" that we are entering a region with some interesting cultures and specific ways of saying things. The classical form of the Arabic language is the language of the Koran. Problems of translatability emerge right from the start where Islam is concerned. Islamic belief is founded on the principle of *iman*. This word is usually translated as "faith," but in fact it is nothing like faith as conceived in a Western sense. A Muslim's belief is founded on a deeply rational persuasion of its rightness, and therefore to a believer in Islam the Western existentialist idea of a "leap of faith" would make no sense at all.

Local oral narrating and performing traditions have long been part of the Middle Eastern culture. Many Muslim Arabs memorize portions of the Koran, and it is not uncommon for devout believers to commit the entire scripture to memory.

Arab oral traditions can perhaps be summed up by the following untranslatable word. *Halca* is an artistic genre so famed – and threatened – that it is now under UNESCO cultural protection. To describe *halca* simply as "storytelling" would do an injustice to this ancient Arab street tradition of improvised song, dance, and story where the audience gathers in a circle around the performers. A renowned *halca* venue is in Jemaa–el Fna Square in Marrakech, Morocco. The Spanish author Juan Goytisolo, a regular resident of the city, describes it eloquently:

The *halca,* the circle of listeners and spectators . . .
forms around the storyteller. . . . The storyteller addresses
these people directly; they are his accomplices. The text
he recites or improvises functions like a score, leaving the
performer a wide margin of freedom. In the oral tradition,
changes in voice and oratorical rhythm, expressions and
gestures, play a fundamental role: even a seemingly sacred
text can be parodied and lowered to a scatological level.
In children's stories and *chansons de geste,* the frequent use of
para-linguistic devices and cynegetic sketches (which evoke
hunting), stresses the magic, power or dramatic aspects of
the episodes being told.

The hero story cycles of the Middle Eastern culture belong in
the same tradition as *alf layla wa layla,* more commonly known to
Westerners as *The Thousand and One Nights*
or *The Arabian Nights.* These stories owe
their origins largely to the storytelling
traditions of the Persian
and Arab worlds. Derived from a
tenth-century Persian book of
folktales called *Hazarafsaneh,* some
of the best-known stories, such as
Aladdin, Sinbad the Sailor, and
Ali Baba and the Forty Thieves
were translated by Englishman
Sir Richard Burton in the
nineteenth century. They are a
valuable source of Middle Eastern
social history across the medieval
Islamic period. Of course the
subtleties of the language are lost in
the translation but the exotic and
romantic imagery is universal
and inspirational.

Arabic

Arabic must surely come at the summit of the world's untranslatable tongues. The Arabic language of the Middle Ages exercised enormous influence throughout Europe, such was the expertise and learning of ancient Arab cultural centers.

In our own time, those classical Arabic terms that have slipped into Western consciousness – the best known being perhaps *jihad* and *fatwa* – are more often than not clumsily expressed or colored in a way that deepens misunderstanding rather than helping intercultural relations. Leaving classical Arabic to one side, we enter the confusing world of a dozen different dialects of colloquial and regional Arabic, nearly all of which reveal centuries of cross-cultural or colonial interference. Brian Whitaker, the Middle Eastern correspondent of the United Kingdom newspaper *The Guardian* provides an enthusiastic insight into the language phenomenon known in North Africa as *frarabic*, a Maghrebian version of *franglais*.

Arabic is certainly a wonderfully expressive language, and I have met Arabs with little education whose feel for its words and their capabilities is absolutely astonishing. But all languages have some weaknesses and, by interchange, can enrich each other. The Algerians are famous – or notorious – for mixing Arabic and French, often in the same sentence, and occasionally even in the same word. One of these hybrids is *haytiste* which combines the Arabic word *hayt* ('wall') with the French *-iste* (as in *artiste*). It describes the sort of young Algerian man – unemployed, bored and, in all probability, up to no good – who hangs around the streets leaning against walls. You won't find it in the dictionary, but you'd be hard pressed to find an eight-letter word in any language more replete with colourful social imagery.

From the same unhappy Algerian background of disenchanted, poor, and unemployed youth, comes *hogra*, the untranslatable Arabic term for that feeling of rage, desperation, and resentment that fills a person or a society faced with a tomorrow as bleak as today.

bukra [*book*-rah] (adverb)

This is the most common time reference in daily use in the Arab world, always qualified by *insh'allah* meaning "God willing." Your Arabic phrasebook will tell you that *bukra* means "tomorrow," but this is not quite accurate. Its real meaning is "an indeterminate time in the future," Indeed it has been said that *bukra* is "like *mañana* in Spanish but without the same sense of urgency." In an article titled *Thinking in Tongues*, Joumana Medlej writes that the Lebanese word for "now" is *hella,* which actually means "'presently,' 'when I'm done,' 'later.'" Medlej comments, "It's hard at this point to tell whether our relaxed way of life seeped into the language or language encouraged the culture to take it easy." Those who have enjoyed the relaxed and civilized atmosphere of working in Arab countries will remember the convivial hours spent sitting with coffee in offices, waiting for the moment when the assurances of *bukra* and *hella* engage with the present.

taarradhin [*tah*-rah-deen] (noun)

Arabic has no word for "compromise" in the sense of reaching an arrangement via struggle and disagreement. But a much happier concept, *taarradhin,* exists in Arabic. It implies a happy solution for everyone, an "I win, you win." It's a way of resolving a problem without anyone losing face.

djinn [djiin] (noun)

To desert Arab people, the *djinn* were a race of spirits to be feared. Just as humans were made from the dust of the earth, the *djinn* were spirits made from fire. They had free will and because of this could roam anywhere they wished, causing mischief and havoc. Early Arabic beliefs gave them the power to change shape, to take possession of a person, or even to appear as beautiful women who would lie with men at night and draw their energy from them. As they were essentially out of control, the *djinn* had to be tackled by Islamic holy men and were usually captured and confined to objects. Hence Aladdin's "genie" of the lamp whom he unwittingly set free! Genie is no more than a Westernization of *djinni,* the singular noun of *djinn.*

halaal [hal-*ahl*] (noun)

Halaal is a term you often hear in Arabic countries. It refers to a wide number of practices and customs that are permitted under Islamic law. Therefore in daily life the word broadly means "permissible," as opposed to *haraam,* which means "forbidden." In non–Arabic speaking countries, the term is used most often with reference to Islamic laws regulating diet and food, especially in the choice and preparation of meat. Pork, for instance, is *haraam.*

hilm il-utat kullu firaan [helm el-o-tot koo-loo fee-rahn] (idiom)

On a more domestic note, this idiom involves cats, such a famous part of Arabic culture. It can be translated as "the dream of cats is all about mice." And the meaning? "To have a one-track mind!"

baksheesh [bak-sheesh] (noun)

This word encompasses a variety of different kinds of giving of small amounts of money and acts as a kind of informal welfare system. If you are wealthy, it is incumbent on you to share the wealth in small ways. This can be done in three main ways. The first as a small reward or tip for a small service rendered. The second usually involves the granting of favors. Examples might include letting you into a historical site after hours, finding you a seat or a sleeper on a train that is "full," or speeding up some bureaucratic process. The last kind of *baksheesh* is alms-giving, an important social custom and a tenet of Islam, whereby the giver is made holy by the action.

haj [*hadj*] (noun)

The *haj* is the pilgrimage to Mecca and is the fifth of the Five Pillars of Islam, the observances that are the foundation of Islam. Every Muslim who is able and can afford to do so is obliged to make the pilgrimage to Mecca at least once in their lifetime and perform certain traditional rites while they are there. The government of Saudi Arabia issues special visas to foreigners for the purpose of the pilgrimage, which takes place during the Islamic month of *Dhu Al-Hijjah*. Entrance to the city itself is forbidden to non-Muslims, as the entire city is holy to Islam. The pilgrim is known as *hajji,* and a person who has completed a pilgrimage may be known by this term for the rest of his life. *Haj* pilgrims are required to dress simply in an *ihram,* a garment made of two sheets of white unhemmed cloth, and a pair of sandals. The *ihram* makes all pilgrims equal in the eyes of Allah, as there is no difference between rich and poor when everyone is dressed the same.

baraka [bah-*rahk*-ah] (noun)

Baraka is a word of several meanings. It can represent a state of heightened consciousness or grace achieved through religious fervor involving prayer and dancing. It can also mean a blessing that can be carried and transferred from one person to another or from an object to a person. It's most often carried by someone who has been on a pilgrimage or has made the *haj* to Mecca. Pilgrims returning from Mecca bring *baraka* in themselves, as well as in objects from holy places. More broadly, a person of character, courage, and selflessness can be considered to possess *baraka*. Its equivalent in Hebrew is *baruch*, which means blessed.

Turkish

T urkey has always had a bit of an identity crisis. Straddling
Europe and Asia, culturally the Turks themselves were one
of the many peoples that made up the Ottoman Empire. The
Turkish dialect is a mixture of Arabic, Persian, and Turkish, and up
until 1923, members of the military, civil, and religious elite spoke
a different language to the lower classes. Led by Mustafa Kemal
Ataturk, the government introduced sweeping language reforms
to "purify" Turkish, making a language that enabled the people in
power to speak to, and be understood by, the people they ruled.
They set out to make the formal Turkish language easier to learn.
Ataturk, determined that the transition to the new language
would take only a few months, traveled throughout Turkey with
chalk and a portable blackboard, personally teaching the new
alphabet in schools, village squares, and other public places.

Cultural confusion and devotion to various religions
has added to Turkish some delightful untranslatable words,
particularly ones laden with spiritual and emotional feeling.

helal [hell-*ahl*] (verb)
> This is an active word that seems to defy all attempts at
> translation. *Helal* is an action, and when you give *helal*
> to someone for something, it means "what I give you is
> rightfully yours, you deserve it so you owe me nothing for it."
> If a person has been fed *helal süt,* their mother has no regrets
> whatsoever for having fed them, they deserve it all. It is almost
> a compliment to the person to whom you give *helal*. You are
> letting them know that they are an honest, upright person.

sütü bozu [soo-too boh-*zook*] (idiom)
> "Bad milk" is the literal translation of this phrase. It is an
> offensive expression that means immorality or a corrupt
> personality. There is also an expression, "human beings are

being fed raw milk," which means that one should not expect
to trust someone immediately. Perhaps the closest that we get
to it in English is the expression "bad egg," although the
French have an expression *soupe au lait,* meaning, "milk soup,"
or short-tempered. It must be said that either expression
certainly adds a bad smell to an insult.

gönül [ger-*nool*] (noun)

This word literally translates as "heart." But it is more than
this, as you can also translate the Turkish words *yürek* and
kalp as "heart." *Gönül* is something deeper. It belongs to
your inner self and the energy that is within you. There is
an element of the hearts of all people being united in your
heart because you wish for their well-being.

denize girse kurutur [*den*–i-say geer-se kuh-ruh-*toor*] (idiom)

This is a wonderful phrase that means something like "he
can't do anything right." However, the Turkish language
renders this sentiment in a more colorful and picturesque way,
literally saying, "he gets dry if he enters the sea."

denize düs en yilana sarilir

[*den*-i-say duss en yee-lan-ah sa-
ruh-*leer*] (idiom)
Another phrase that evokes
imagery of the sea, this one
literally translates, "if you
fall into the sea, hold onto
a snake." It highlights the
understanding that you
will accept help in any
way, no matter what it
looks like, if you are in
a bad situation.

Persian

I s this language called Persian or is it called Farsi? Spoken today primarily in Iran and Afghanistan, the debate over what to call this language goes as far back as sixth–century B.C. The early Persians lived in a region called Fars, which was known to the Greeks as Persis. When Islam was introduced to Iran around the fifth century, the Arabic name for Persia was Farsi, and this was the name given to the language. In Iran, the language is commonly known as Farsi. Elsewhere in the Western world, it is known as Persian.

chador [*chuhd*-ur] (noun)

The *chador* is the veil worn by women that covers their whole body and dress. This word literally means "tent." This kind of dress comes embodied with the ideas of female seclusion and modesty. The widespread wearing of the *chador* was revived in Iran in the 1970s by Ayatollah Khomeini, responding to the Koranic request for modesty in dress.

daste kasi ra dar hana gozashtah [das-teh ka-si *rah* dah ha-na go-*zash*-tah] (idiom)

Literally to "put someone's hand in the water," this phrase has a very unlikely meaning, one that we might never guess at. When spoken by a Persian, it means to involve someone in difficulties to the point where you embarrass them.

kæs nækha-ræd posht e mæn joz na-khon e ængosht e mæn [*kaz* nakh-*how*-rahd *posht* ay mann joz nowr-hon ay an-*gosht* ay mann] (idiom)

The verbatim translation of this idiom is "no one will scratch my back except my own finger." In contrast to the English phrase "I'll scratch your back, if you scratch mine," the sentiment behind this expression is that you can achieve all you want in life if you rely on yourself rather than others.

dastu del baz boodan [dast-o del *bahz* boo-dan] (idiom)

This phrase literally means "the opening of hand and heart." It describes the idea of being free with your money, not being stingy, and having a generosity toward others.

tazieh [*ta*-zi-eh] (noun)

From the Arabic word *taziat,* which means "to mourn," this is a ritual play, usually tragic and heroic, performed each year on the anniversaries of the funerals of religious *imams.* The practice is widespread in all parts of Iran with Shiite majority. Most of the players are amateur, and men play the role of women. They may omit or add something to the original text. Sometimes the audience helps the process, playing the role of chorus by clapping and reciting some parts of the play. This seems to be the Persian–specific version of the Arabic *halca.*

taarof [ta-*ah*-rof] (noun)

In Persian culture it is customary to offer food and drink to someone when they come to visit you in your home. *Taarof* roughly translates as accepting someone's hospitality, taking something that you may not want so that you don't offend them. A host might say "*Taarof nakon,*" meaning, "Don't just sit there, help yourself." In response someone might say, "*Taarof nemikonam,*" meaning, "I'm not just sitting here."

Chapter 6

African Languages

here are many languages and dialects across the African continent. Languages that have originated from Bantu include Hausa, Yoruba, Zulu, and, perhaps the most widely spoken of all, Swahili.

Swahili is a rich language that includes words taken from Arabic, Hindi, Persian, Turkish, Portuguese, and English. The word *swahili* itself was used by early Arab visitors to the African coast and means "the coast." Ultimately it came to be applied to the language.

Lingala, a northern African tongue, is atonal and depends entirely on pronunciation for meaning. As you can imagine, this poses all kinds of misunderstandings and problems for the language in a written form. *Mbula* can mean either "rain" or "year"; *nguba* could mean "shield" or "peanut"; and, more alarmingly, *moto* can mean "person," "head," or "fire."

Swahili time is a concept that is understood all over Africa as well as in South Pacific island languages. Time for the Swahili culture starts at sunrise, unlike the Arab world, where it starts at sunset, and the Western world, where it starts at midnight. As East Africa is located on the Equator, sunrise happens each day at 6 A.M. and is known as "zero o'clock," *saa moja asubuhi* is one o'clock in the morning but to a Westerner it is 7 A.M. Be sure then, when you need to be somewhere while visiting an African country, that you find out whether you are speaking in Swahili time or some other kind of time.

kanga (Swahili) [*kahn*-ga] (noun)

The *kanga* is the traditional printed cloth worn
by women that is encoded with a proverb or
message. They are worn in pairs, one is often
worn over a dress or a skirt to protect the
clothing underneath, and the other
might be worn as a head covering or
tied as a sling to carry a baby. Women
can speak volumes to the community
without saying a word. *Kanga* proverbs
include *mdhaniaye ndiye kumbe siye,* literally
translating as "the one whom you think is
the right one is the wrong one," or in other
words, "you are barking up the wrong tree";
moyo wangu Sultani, cha mtu sikitamani,
literally, "my heart is like Sultan,
I don't long for anybody else's property," or, "I
am satisfied"; and *siku ya kufa nyani miti yote
huteleza,* "the day a monkey is destined to die,
all trees get slippery," or, "there is no escaping
one's fate."

natondi yo (Lingala) [*na*-ton-di yor] (verb)

In the Lingala language there is no word for "thank you"
except *melesi,* transliterated from French. But the verb *kotonda*
– "to be full" – is used in the expression *natondi yo* to convey
the sentiment, "I thank you."

safari (Swahili) [sa-*fah*-ee] (noun)

Safari is not an unfamiliar word in English. Conjuring up
pictures of pith helmets, zebras, jeeps, and groups of tourists,
this word derives from Swahili, from the verb *kusafiri,* which
means to travel. In some Western slang, *safari* has come to
mean a journey of any kind, not just one to view wildlife.

oruko lonro ni (Yoruba) [or-roo -ko lon-ro nee] (idiom)

It is a long-held belief among people of the Yoruba language that *oruko lonro ni* – "names affect behavior." A child with the name *Sumala,* meaning "thief," would go on to steal anything that wasn't tied down. If parents make a bad choice of name at the birth of their child, the only way to deal with the problem is to rechristen the child.

bado (Swahili) [*bah*-doh] (idiom)

This word appears to translate transparently, as one of the first a child comes to understand and make use of, the word that parents learn to dread because they hear it so much: "no!" However, *bado* has a deeper meaning and is actually used to say "no" when it is theoretically possible that the action may occur in the future. Employed to answer questions such as "Will you buy a new car?" or "Do you have children?" it means "No, not yet." Another Swahili phrase, *sasa hivi,* translates literally as "soon" or "right away," but be careful as "just now" might mean several hours in the future to the South African speaking with you.

palatyi (Bantu) [pa-la-tee-yeh] (noun)

The West African Bantu people talk of a supernatural being thought to haunt their land. It's called the *palatyi,* or "plat-eye prowl" and is a mythical animal-like ghost that comes and scratches on your door on cold, dark nights. What could possibly be more frightening if you live in a remote village and you hear something in the night?

bacheque (Lingala) [bah-check] (noun)

This word describes the local "man on the street," the one who lives on nothing but his wits. The closest English translation might be "con artist." This is the man in Kinshasa who will sell you a car (especially when yours has mysteriously disappeared the day before) or organize a night out on the town for you or a tour of the local sights. Wearing a loud shirt and the best designer watch, *bacheque* serve a vital brokering purpose when the formal economy has dramatically broken down. They change currency, establish market prices, and give the capital its characteristic feel.

ilunga (Tshiluba) [ee-lun-ga] (noun)
This word from the Tshiluba language of the Republic of Congo has topped a list drawn up with the help of one thousand translators as the most untranslatable word in the world. It describes a person who is ready to forgive any transgression a first time and then to tolerate it for a second time, but never for a third time.

ngando (Dzokanga) [gee-a-doh] (noun)
This word means "crocodile" in the Dzokanga language of the Congo area of Africa, but it ia also used to speak about a tram or bus driver and seems to translate literally as "frogman." What this implies about such professions, I'll leave to your imagination!

Chapter 7

Asian Languages

Westerners who have lived or worked in Asia are all too
aware that the cultural gap between East and West can
be daunting, if not completely baffling at times. The
differences are not only profound but ancient.

No conceptual difference could illustrate this more than the
Eastern approach to time relationships. Chinese, for instance,
has no tenses and lacks the simple linear approach to time found
in Western languages. Temporal relations are treated as "aspects"
or ways of juxtaposing things, which are much more subtle
and alterable. Events are not lined up one-by-one through a
rigorously logical sequence but may be visualized, so to speak,
simultaneously.

Eastern cultures are highly complex in day-to-day personal or
working relationships, too, involving careful positioning of oneself
according to social codes that are mostly unwritten. In a lot of
American business literature we find advice on the tricky issue of
avoiding unintentional offense with Asian colleagues. Could it be
that the British, with their tradition of hiding their feelings and
never quite saying what they mean, find more kinship with
Eastern attitudes, such as the Japanese virtue of *enryo,* "restraint"
or "reserve"?

However, the British stiff upper lip does not protect against
miscommunication or mistranslation. Dr. Henry Zhao, a modern
Chinese specialist, related this story:

> Chinese are well-known for their modesty, and
> Chinese diplomats more so. A particular diplomat
> in London brought his wife to a banquet and the
> host, the British Foreign Minister, accompanied
> by a UK-trained translator, greeted them at the
> doorway. The Minister said, "Your wife is

gorgeous." His translator handled that well.
The diplomat felt the need to be modest and
said *"Nali! Nali!"* The word *nali* in Chinese usually
means "where," but when responding to
a compliment it literally means, "How could that
be?" and should be translated as "We are flattered."
But the poor translator only remembered his first-
year lessons, and rendered it as "Where? Where?"
With a sharp English wit, the Foreign Minister
said, "Oh, everywhere."

The Japanese people not only distinguish between different
types of reality but have a distinctively Japanese view of
"sincerity," for which they have no exact word of their own.
Makoto is often used to translate "sincerity," but in Japan it means
speaking with sensitivity to other people's feelings. This is quite
different from the Western notion of a "sincerity" that honestly
declares what the speaker believes or feels in the interests of
truthfulness. In Japan such rudeness would be unthinkable!

Andrew Horvat, author of *Japanese Beyond Words,* provides
some further fascinating insights into the cultural gaps:

Last week, I came across a Japanese book devoted
to the history of just ten expressions: *shakai* –
(society), *kojin* – (individual), *kindai* – (modern),
bi – (beauty), *ren'ai* – (romantic love), *sonzai* –
(existence), *shizen* – (nature), *kenri* – (rights), *jiyu* –
(freedom), and *kare/kanojo* – (he/she). Every one
of these expressions, all borrowings from European
languages, took decades to find Japanese equivalents.
Suddenly, I understood why the nineteenth-century
educator, Yukichi Fukuzawa, who helped translate
into Japanese the first two words from the above
list, made it onto the Y10,000 bill.

The following untranslatables illustrate some of the pitfalls
and delights of entering into a more Eastern way of seeing things.

Chinese

I t took Joseph Needham and his Cambridge colleagues over twenty years (and five volumes of *Science and Civilisation in China*) to demonstrate that most of the modern ideas the West considers its own had been long ago thought of by Chinese thinkers and experimenters. Paradoxically, the story of modern China is one of the dominance of Western social and scientific thought and technology, and many ancient traditions have been depreciated and dismissed. But as we shall see, the mixtures and contradictions between the old and the new are as potent as ever.

The different structure of Chinese, which builds words through combinations of pictures or ideograms, has been refining the concepts that affect almost everything they do and say for over four thousand years. Chinese has seven major language groups, though the main dialects used in China are Mandarin and Cantonese. As the predominant language spoken in mainland China, classical Mandarin is like Latin to the ancient world, acting as the traditional tongue of scholarly works and communication. Cantonese may be considered a more modern Chinese language, hence it is spoken in the Westernized regions of China, such as the Southeast provinces of Guandong and Guangxi, also in overseas Chinese communities in Australia, Europe, and America.

The language barrier between Westerners and the Chinese is perhaps more of a culture barrier. As Chinese culture is based on Confucian principles directing all levels of social relations, along with Taoist principles of conceiving the world and its infinite laws of change, the barriers to understanding are huge. However, some things were easier to export from China. One of our common modern words is a simple corruption of the original Chinese *Kê Tsiap,* the name of a spicy sauce brought back to Europe in the seventeenth century. The word? "Ketchup."

The following examples reveal some of the cultural challenges of living in China, and offer slightly more difficulty, if not impossibility, in translation.

tao (dao) (Mandarin) [*dah*-oh] (noun)

Tao is the central concept of the Taoist tradition, usually translated as "the Way." It is said that without an understanding of *Tao*, it is impossible to understand Chinese culture. However, when we try to address this challenge, we run up against obstacles such as the very opening line of the classic Taoist text, the *Dao De Jing*, written by the greatest Chinese philosopher Lao-tzu two and a half thousand years ago: "The *Tao* that can be spoken of is not the eternal *Tao*." Well, if we cannot speak of it, we cannot translate it. The author Alan Watts, who spent a lifetime bringing Eastern concepts to a Western audience, writes of this problem, "I prefer not to translate the word *Tao* at all because to us *Tao* is a sort of nonsense syllable indicating the mystery that we can never understand."

ming zhi (Mandarin) [ming-*zhee*] (noun)

This term, based on the elements *ming*, meaning "dark, dim, otherworld" and *zhi*, meaning "paper," refers to "ghost money," which in parts of China is sold in bundles for ritual burning. The Chinese burn *ming zhi* in metal containers at the side of the road, or outside temples, businesses, shops, or by street stalls. Printed on the money are the characters for Happiness, Peace, Good Fortune, and so on, depending on what you wish to send to the gods, ghosts, or spirits. The burning of the money will ward off angry spirits or satisfy a "hungry ghost" from the underworld so it won't bother you or your family.

renao (Mandarin) [ren-*ah*-oh] (adjective)

This word literally means "hot" but includes the additional meanings of "noisy," "making noise," and "stirring up trouble." Not overlaid with negative connotation, in China the term is a positive, implying "lively, festive, happy, noisy" – especially, noisy! The Chinese do not have the same response to noise as Westerners, and are even attracted by it, which explains the loud music in stores and restaurants, as well as the very *renao* practice of setting off firecrackers. The Chinese like to live close together, and enjoy the excitement of a city, which is also very *renao*.

feng shui (Mandarin) [feng-shoo-*ay*] (noun)

Literally, "wind water," this is the study and practice of arranging your life in correct alignment with surrounding nature, in particular the location and furnishing of your house. Now so fashionable in the West, it barely needs more comment.

guanxi (Mandarin) [*gwan*-shee] (noun)

This is one of the essential ways of getting things done in traditional Chinese society. To build up good *guanxi,* you do things for people such as give them gifts, take them to dinner, or grant favors. Conversely, you can also "use up" your *guanxi* with someone by calling in favors owed. Once a favor is done, an unspoken obligation exists. Maybe because of this, people often try to refuse gifts, because, sooner or later, they may have to repay the debt. However the bond of *guanxi* is rarely acquitted, because once the relationship exists, it sets up an endless process that can last a lifetime.

qi (chi) (Mandarin) [chee] (noun)

Qi or chi is a fundamental and untranslatable word that affects many aspects of Chinese life and society from health, sex, and longevity, to social relations, enterprise, work, and play. It is perhaps the most basic concept of Chinese traditional medicine. Here it refers to something like a life energy, an energy in movement, with a direction or tendency. Matter and energy are conceptualized as aspects of the same thing. The task of healing therapies is to gather a person's *qi* and then direct it as required. The measurement of *qi,* or of different types of *qi,* indicates your "life strength" and how much respect you are due in wider social terms.

yinyang (Cantonese) [*yeen*-yeung] (noun)

A fundamental concept in Chinese culture. The closest meaning in English is "female, male" but *yin* also means "soft, gentle, implicit" and *yang* "hard, strong, explicit." For example, female, water, and the moon are *yin,* and male, mountain, and the sun are *yang.* Both *yin* and *yang* are symbols of strength of an opposing nature, and optimal strength is the combination of *yin* and *yang,* which must be harmoniously balanced to sustain all forms of life. If you are ill, it could be understood that there is too much *yin,* "cold," or *yang,* "hot," in your body, and to cure the illness, *yinyang* must be rebalanced through various means such as herbal medicine, acupuncture, or exercises like *taiji* and *qigong.*

zhongyong (Mandarin) [zohng-*yong*] (noun)

This is another fundamental concept in the Chinese culture and philosophy. *Zhong* means "middle, mean" and *yong* means "ordinary, normal, simple." From the title of one of the four greatest Chinese classics, the closest English translation is "the doctrines of the mean." *Zhongyong* emphasizes the avoidance of all forms of extreme based on common sense. Moderation, compromise, and a sense of proportion in any aspect of life are valued against radicalism, rigidity, and extremism.

gagung (Cantonese) [ga-*gung*] (noun)

As a result of the one-child policy in China, the number of surplus males is now over a hundred million. This sad term, which means "bare sticks," or "bare branches," refers to the men who are unlikely to marry or to have families because of the skewed sex ratios.

jingjie (Mandarin) [jing-gee] (noun)

Jingjie refers mainly to the highest moral and spiritual state. The Chinese believe that all human beings are good by nature. But good nature can be corrupted during the course of life owing to both human weaknesses and evil influences in society. So education is important, the primary aim of which is to cultivate a person to be a moral being and to reach the highest *jingjie.*

Japanese

J apanese is comparable to a complex secret code, designed to protect the elaborate workings of Japanese society from rude outsiders and their clodhopping foreign ways. Only when you've cracked the code – that is, you can speak Japanese – can you begin to understand the country's unique culture and access its secrets. Although this is true to some extent of any language, Japanese linguistic expression and psychology are interwoven to such an astonishing degree that if you pick almost any word, you have the germ of a cultural seminar.

Central to traditional, hierarchical Japanese society is the concept of *wa,* meaning "harmony." Harmonious relations are *de rigueur* in all aspects of life, including government and business. The delicacy of the Japanese language, with its characteristically vague and soft expressions, helps to keep the boat from rocking and ensure no one is offended. A Westerner who tries to jolly proceedings along with some crass idea of telling it like it is, is likely to bring on retreat accompanied by a shudder of distaste. If in doubt, apologize in advance for the offence you're almost bound to cause.

One of the most remarkable and remarked on aspects of Japanese life and language is its emphasis on aesthetics. This cultural obsession with beauty has given rise to a richly expressive vocabulary that puts English to shame – our untranslatables merely skim the surface. Consider *myo, yugen,* and *shibui. Myo* refers to the mysterious spirit that imbues the truly beautiful. *Yugen* expresses the mystery and subtlety that lie beneath the surface of things. *Shibui* embraces both *myo* and *yugen* and is a more generic term, epitomizing classic Japanese simplicity. Whether being steeped in expressive vocabulary makes the Japanese more artistic in general is a moot point. They certainly have bags of style.

yoko meshi
[*yoh*-koh *mesh*-ee]
(noun)
"As an
untranslatable,
this one ranks
high on my list of
favorites. I could not
improve on the background
given by commentator
Boyé Lafayette de Mente
about this beautiful word,
yoko meshi. Taken literally, *meshi*
means 'boiled rice' and *yoko*
means 'horizontal,' so combined you
get 'a meal eaten sideways.' This is how the Japanese
define the peculiar stress induced by speaking a foreign
language: *yoko* is a humorous reference to the fact that
Japanese is normally written vertically, whereas most foreign
languages are written horizontally. How do English-speakers
describe the headache of communicating in an alien tongue?
I don't think we can, at least not with as much ease."

aware [ah-*wah*-ray] (noun)
An awareness and appreciation of the ephemeral beauty of the
world. The seasons change, the cherry blossom gently falls, the
crops are planted, grow, and die. *Aware* is that poignant
sensation one has of time passing, of the inevitable cycle of life
and death. From the noun comes the idiom *mono-no-aware*.
Roughly translated as "enjoying the sadness of life," it's that
bittersweet, vaguely poetic feeling you get around dusk, on a
long train journey, looking out at the driving rain . . . a few
autumn leaves still clinging to your coat.

hai [*hye*] (noun)

The smallest words can cause the greatest misunderstandings. *Hai* is a constant source of problems in East–West relations. The closest we have to it is an encouraging "ummm" combined with a sympathetic nod of the head. It means, "Yes, I am listening to you and I understand what you are saying." What it certainly doesn't mean is, "Yes, I agree with you." There lies the rub.

nemawashi [nem-ah-*wash*-ee] (noun)

Literally meaning "revolving the roots," *nemawashi* describes the long process that permeates the ranks of a Japanese company as it contemplates a new proposal or action. Since the Japanese characteristically function as a group, *nemawashi* is likely to involve almost everyone in the company. As an outsider with a vested interest, patience is your best asset. Aggressive persuasion tactics and a snap decision are out of the question.

tatemae [*tah*-tay-mye] (noun)

A term often translated as "form," but it also has the specific cultural meaning of "the reality that everyone professes to be true, even though they may not privately believe it." For privately held views, the Japanese have a different term, *honne,* meaning, "the reality that you hold inwardly to be true, even though you would never admit it publicly." The British civil servant muttering the reproach "bad form, old boy" over a drink in the club, may be expressing something very close to the quality of *tatamae*.

sempai [*sem*-pye] (noun)

Simply translated as "senior," it is the highest honor to be *sempai* in the vertically arranged world of Japanese society. The position is enduring – your *sempai* at school or college remains worthy of respect and deference for life. More than a mere "mentor," a *sempai* is never free of the special obligation to watch out for and advise his or her juniors, whether at work or in their personal lives.

shibui [shib-*oo*-ee] (noun)

Shibui describes an aesthetic that only time can reveal.
As we become older and more marked by the riches of
life's experience, we radiate with a beauty that stems from
becoming fully ourselves. The term can be applied to almost
anything – a landscape, a house, or even a piece of aged wood
can be deemed fine art.

hanko [*hahn*-koe] (noun)

The Japanese system of writing, originally borrowed from the
Chinese, uses several thousand complicated ideograms that
are extremely difficult to master both in reading and writing.
A *hanko* is a stamp carved with your name as an ideogram,
which is used as a personal seal. This seal traditionally appears
in place of your signature and it is still widely used today for
all official documents. Paintings and other art are also
"stamped" with an artist's *hanko*.

wabi-sabi [*wab*-ee-*sab*-ee] (noun)

Meaning something like "tranquil," *wabi* is one of the most
important words in the extensive aesthetic vocabulary of
Japanese. Unless something has *wabi*, it simply isn't Japanese.
The first people involved with *wabi-sabi,* that is, the aesthetic
system that places *wabi* at its center, were Zen Buddhists – tea
masters, priests, and monks, who emphasized a direct, intuitive
insight into transcendental truth. Therefore *wabi-sabi* is the
beauty of things imperfect, impermanent, incomplete, modest,
and humble.

kokusaijin [*kok*-oo-sye-jin] (noun)

Another noun that represents Japan's untranslatable worldview is *kokusaijin* literally meaning "an international person"
but referring exclusively to Japanese citizens who are able
to get along with foreigners. "Cosmopolitan" is the closest
English equivalent, but this word connotes someone who
speaks foreign languages and knows a lot about foreign
countries and cultures. A Japanese *kokusaijin* may be an
ordinary person with a flexible and open personality.

East/Southeast Asian Languages

As we travel south through Asia, we come across many different cultures, but most are infused with the same Eastern philosophy and beauty of expression we have already encountered. Of course, different cultures reflect their way of living through their language. It certainly says something about the local diet that the Hanunoo language of the Philippines has ninety different words for rice!

Also based on this commonly eaten foodstuff, the Indonesian idiom *nasi sudah menjadi bubur* literally translates as "the rice has already become porridge." *Bubur* is made by boiling rice to the point that it becomes mushy, like porridge. It is eaten with vegetables, various meat, and sauces. The concept is that once the rice has turned to porridge, there is no turning back. It is too late as the process cannot be reversed – the rice is now porridge. There is no crying over spilled milk in Indonesia! Here are some more words exploring the expression and ways of understanding specific to Southern and Southeast Asian cultures.

mai pen rai (Thai) [my-pen-*lye*] (idiom)

This is the most common Thai response to a difficulty – literally, "never mind," "no problem," or "it can't be helped." This is the verbal equivalent of an open-handed shoulder shrug, which has its basis in the Buddhist notion of karma. This will help any traveler to understand the sometimes *laissez-faire* attitude to delayed buses and other general day-to-day problems and inconveniences.

jung (Korean) [*yung*] (noun)

This word in Korean represents a special feeling or a relationship that one person has with another that is stronger than mere "love" and can only often be proved by having survived a huge argument with someone. It is a word that represents a feeling that can never die, and is unlike love in this way. It highlights the difference between the Korean concept of love and the Western romantic ideal of love.

gotong-royong (Indonesian) [*got*-ong-*roi*-ong] (noun)
Indonesians use *royong* to mean "mutual cooperation" or, more precisely, the relationship between a group of people who are committed to accomplish a task of mutual benefit. The word goes back to the days when small farmers worked together and used a common area in the center of the village or town for grazing their cattle. The word is almost always used in conjunction with *gotong-royong*, which means, "to carry a heavy burden together," and it has been co-opted

by politicians and used to convey the sense that the common good is more important than the individual.

jai yen (Thai) [jye *yen*] (noun)
Thai people are quite reserved, but their language alerts us to their hidden emotional depths. *Jai* literally means "heart," but it may also mean "mind." There are hundreds of Thai phrases that use the word *jai* to describe many kinds of emotional

states and mental feelings. *Jai yen* translates literally as "cool heart" and is something everyone tries to maintain, an easy going calmness. Most Thai people hate raised voices, visible irritation, and confrontation of any kind. In many ways, this is part of the Buddhist philosophy that many Thai people follow. In Thai, your heart can be described in many ways, including hot, black, strange, or little.

nunchi (Korean) [*noon*-chee] (noun)

This word is bound up in the social niceties and customs of interaction that are second nature to the people of Asia. *Nunchi* refers to a sort of "sixth sense," an intrinsic understanding of the person with whom you are interacting, and is essential for evaluating another person's hidden feelings and staying one step ahead of offending them.

khian duay meu, lop duay thao (Thai) [*kee*-un doo-ay meu, *lop* doo-ay taow] (idiom)

Parts of the body have spiritual significance and hierarchy to Thai people. The head is the highest part of the body and it is rude to touch a Thai person's head. The feet are the lowest part of the body and it is similarly rude to point to things with your foot. This Thai idiom is steeped in this cultural understanding and literally means "write with the hand, erase with the foot." It refers to a person who wipes out a good deed by immediately following it with a bad one.

nop (Laotian) [*norp*] (noun)

Very similar to the Thai greeting *wai,* this word embodies the respectfulness and politeness that is second nature to the Southeast Asian community. It is accompanied by a prayerlike palms–together greeting gesture. You should *nop* back to someone if they *nop* you in greeting, but you should refrain if a child does it to you.

ramai (Indonesian) [*rahm*-eye] (noun)

People on the island of Bali tend to do things in groups and this word *ramai* has been adopted into standard Indonesian from the original Balinese *rame,* meaning a "crowded, bustling, chaotic social environment." *Ramai* encapsulates one of the main social values of Bali. Most activities, from fishing to fetching firewood and cooking, generally involve a big group of people, usually more than is strictly necessary, and lots of conversation, bustle, and noise.

sayang (Filipino) [sye-yang] (noun)

The closest English translation for a word like *sayang* is an expression such as "what a waste!" but it has more feelings associated with the gravity of the loss than this evokes. It involves a deep sadness or longing for something lost, and feelings of love, compassion, and empathy all enter into this. In another context, the word infers these emotive aspects and it can be a term of endearment like "love," or "sweetheart," or "dear." Koreans have an equivalent for this word, *han,* which is similarly loaded with meaning.

talkin (Indonesian) [*tulk*-in] (noun)

In Indonesia, a religious and spiritual speech called *talkin* refers to whispering instructions in the ear of the dying. Co-opted into the language from Arabic, traditionally these *talkin* are also read at the end of the funeral service to remind the deceased about the answers to give when questioned by the angels of death. In both Hindu and Buddhist traditions, there is a concentration on how to live in order to achieve a propitious incarnation. There is also a concentration on the transition and what can be said to the dying person to help make the experience a positive one.

ada udang di balik batu (Indonesian) [*ud*-dar *oo*-dung *dee baa*-lick *baa*-too] (idiom)

If an Indonesian person said to you *ada udang di balik batu,* you may get slightly confused as they have remarked, "There is a prawn under every rock." The general meaning of the phrase is "there's a hidden catch" or "there are hidden intentions behind what that person is saying."

Indian Languages

T here are fifteen offical languages in India and around seven hundred minor languages or dialects. All currency and ninety percent of government documents bear the scripts of these fifteen languages. These fifteen languages which include Tamil, Kannada, Malayalam, Telegu, Sanskrit, Pali, Hindi, Urdu, Punajabi, Gujarati, Bengali, Marathi, Kashmir, Sindhi, Konkani, Rajasthani, Assamese, and Oriya. Hindi and Urdu are widely spoken and understood everywhere. Urdu is also the official language of Pakistan.

Many Indian words, such as *yoga, khaki, sari, bindi,* and *jodphur,* have already been assimilated into English and other global languages even if the meaning has changed along the way.

masala chai (Urdu) [ma-sa-lah chye] (noun)

> *Chai* in many languages is the term used for tea. It originates from the Chinese word for tea, *cha.* (Hence the English colloquialism "Fancy a cup of char?") Today, *chai* is a general term for a spiced milk tea that is sweetened, and the proper term for this spiced tea is *masala chai, masala* being an Indian word meaning any spice blend. *Chai* is a beverage that is more popular in India than coffee is in the United States. It is available on every street corner from vendors called *chai-valas.* These *chai-valas* carry pots of *chai* and serve it with lots of sugar in freshly fired earthen cups that are discarded after use. It is also a family tradition in India to welcome guests with cups of *chai.* And each family has their own recipe and preparation method.

varna (Hindi) [*vah*-nah] (noun)

> The caste system is the reality of Indian culture and it reaches into all areas of social, religious, and spiritual experience. It has evolved from *varna,* meaning, "color," and originally was only an occupational grouping that roughly corresponded to social classes of society. The classical varnas are *Brahmin,*

meaning, "priest–intellectual," *Kshatriya,* meaning, "warrior," and *Shudra,* meaning, "laborer." In classical times you chose your *varna.* What operates today in Indian culture is actually *jati,* a specialized subgroup that is created out of language, geographical area, and traditional occupation. It splinters social groups and does not foster a larger vision or a culture of bettering oneself through choice. Your caste determines who you will marry, most of your social interactions, and your spirituality.

oont kis karwat baithta hai (Urdu) [*unt* kiss kah-vat bye-tha *hye*] (proverb)

This Urdu proverb, literally meaning, "Let us see which way the camel sits," is evocative of the desert region where camels are the main means of transport. It is said that during a desert sandstorm, you can always tell which direction the wind is blowing by the way that the camel sits. Of course, the clever camel always sits facing a direction that will protect its eyes and nostrils from the sand whipped up by the storm. Then the

camel rider can take cover behind the camel's body. The closest that we get to the meaning in English is probably "Let's see which way the wind blows."

deva (Sanskrit) [*deh*-va] (noun)

This literally means "shining one," and the word is masculine, the feminine is *devi*. They are minor gods and goddesses of the pantheon of the Hindi religion, such as Indra, Agni, and Vayu. However, anyone who accumulates enough good karma may be elevated to the position of a *deva* in *swarga,* the Hindu heaven. They are helpers and illuminators, *vidhvanso hi deva,* literally, "he who gives knowledge." They are similar to Western ideas of guardian angels.

tail dekho tail ki dhaara dekho (Urdu, Hindi, and Punjabi) [*tayl* dee-ko tayl kee dah-ra dee-ko] (proverb)

This proverb means "watch the oil and the way its flow drops." However, this phrase is often used in a political or business context and indicates that some extravigilant observation and attention is required.

rall mil bhenan ikki paaee (Punjabi) [*ral* mil pen-na ick-kee by-ee] (proverb)

This is a popular saying that describes that uncanny ability some people have to promote themselves. Literally, it means "sisters got together and gave twenty-one (rupees)." But, of course, there is a story that illuminates it. There once were three sisters. The first sister married into a rich family and was very quiet and tolerant. The second sister married into a poor family and was very talkative and boastful. The third sister was getting married and it's customary that the other brothers and sisters give money as gifts. The rich sister had twenty rupees and the poor one had only one rupee. Cleverly, the second sister took it upon herself to collect the money. She then presented the gift to the bride exclaiming loudly for all to hear, "The sisters got together and gave twenty-one rupees."

dil baagh baagh ho giya (Urdu and Punjabi) [*dil* bahg bahg ho gay-ah] (proverb)

Literally this means "my heart became a garden garden," and it is used to express overwhelming joy.

eid pichhon tanba phookna? (Punjabi) [*ee*-da pee-tchon tan-ba poo-kan-na] (proverb)

The Eid moon is an important event in India and has spawned numerous phrases, proverbs, and customs. The literal meaning of this proverb is "Are we going to burn the wrapping sheet after Eid?" Often Indian people buy new clothes or give gifts on the Eid as it is considered to be a lucky occasion. Culturally this phrase means that it is no use doing something after the event has already occurred – so, it's no use buying new clothes or gifts after the Eid celebrations have taken place. It's just not lucky.

dhobi (Urdu) [*doh*-bee] (noun)

In India, no one goes to a laundry to have their clothes cleaned. If they don't do their own they send it out to a *dhobi*, for which the closest equivalent might be "washerman" or "washerwoman." The *dhobi* will take the washing out to the *dhobi ghat* or public washing place – a particular spot on the bank of a river is traditional – and it will be thoroughly scrubbed, rinsed, and beaten and then taken to a local ironing shed before coming back in pristine condition. For readers of *Harry Potter* the role of a *dhobi* may not seem a million miles away from that of J. K. Rowling's creation, Dobby the House Elf.

purdah (Urdu) [*per*-dah] (noun)

This word is from the Urdu word *paradah* meaning "veil" or "curtain." Traditionally, this is a curtain or screen used mainly to keep women separated from men or strangers. The Hindu or Muslim system of sex segregation is practiced especially by women in seclusion. It is also used as a word to indicate social seclusion, such as the phrase "artists living in luxurious *purdah.*"

Chapter 8

Ancient and Classical Languages

I t is impossible to speak English without speaking Greek, as Dr. John Karalas demonstrates in the following paragraph from *The Genesis of Classical Drama*, composed entirely of words of Greek origin.

> The prologue, the theme, and the epilogue comprised the trilogy of drama while synthesis, analysis, and synopsis characterised the phraseology of the text. The syntax and phraseology used by scholars, academicians, and philosophers in their rhetoric had many grammatical idioms and idiosyncrasies.

Our intellectual debt to Greek is without question, and even the Romans bowed handsomely to Greek culture. They Latinized a huge number of terms, especially those relating to the refinement of thought, expression, rhetoric, and language generally. A nicely untranslatable example of what linguists call "a rhetorical device" is the word *accismus,* from the Greek *akkismos,* meaning "coyness" or "affectation." This refers to how we may refuse something in a slightly dramatic way to show that we would really rather like to have it. "Oh, no, I couldn't possibly take the last piece, delicious as it was ... and my favorite dessert of all. No, I simply couldn't. Well ..."

The ancient Greeks not only had many ideas and concepts that were quite particular to them and not easily translated into modern terms, but also had a long tradition of uniquely Greek feelings. The Romans, in their turn, gave us town planning, sophisticated techniques of construction, military organization and, in due course, carried by the Christian church on the back of their Empire, the European interlanguage of Vulgar or Medieval Latin. It was this that preserved the linguistic influence of both ancient Greek and Latin in the West to the time of the Renaissance and into this day.

We often forget that other traditions persisted throughout those centuries of the so-called Dark Ages, a time nonetheless of extraordinary cultural vigor and richness. Who thinks of the Visigoths as anything other than barbaric invaders of the Roman Empire? Yet their exquisite art and architecture is a bridge between the classical and the medieval, preserved but overlooked in their ancient kingdoms of northern Spain. One culture in particular that is now reclaiming its rightful place in history is the Celtic tradition, including Gaelic and other Celtic languages.

The Celtic church, at its height around the fifth century A.D., filled the vacuum left by the collapse of Roman rule, sending its missionaries to establish centers of learning all over Europe. It has even been persuasively argued that the Celts "saved civilization." We shall see from our Gaelic untranslatables just how enduring their world vision was, nourishing a way of life that endured right up to the twentieth century in the farthest fringes of Europe.

Linguistically speaking, at the root of all these great traditions stands the legendary pre-Christian civilization of ancient India, with its profound culture explored and expressed through the medium of Sanskrit, and subsequently distributed all over Europe and Asia Minor. All the Indo-European family of tongues owe their origin to Sanskrit and its civilization. We shall see how some of the highest and deepest mysteries of existence found untranslatable names in this language.

Greek

W hat Greeks are always keen to tell you – and there are whole teams of academic linguists looking into this claim – is that you can "feel" things in Greek that are unknown in other languages. Greeks have always had feelings and emotions that nobody else has articulated. In *The Untranslatable Self,* a study of Greek-English bilinguals, Alexia Panayiotou concludes that, "(1) certain emotion terms exist only in specific languages and are therefore untranslatable; and (2) there are emotion terms, that, although linguistically translatable, are culturally untranslatable."

Take "love," for instance. A simple word that in English can mean almost anything. The Greeks knew better and had at least three words for "love." Centuries of debate, from Plato onward, have since taken place around the fine distinctions of *agape, eros,* and *imeros,* which arguably mean "brotherly love," "sexual love," and something entirely untranslatable.

But there is plenty more that the Greeks had words for. What about forgotten stirrings like *thymos,* meaning, "spiritedness"? Certainly we could all do with a bit more of that. If we can't muster up *thymos,* would a little *orge* suffice instead, or is that too severe a prospect? And who among us can honestly say we have recently been feeling *thambos*? Perhaps we have simply been overcome by *anomia,* or overwhelmed by a sense of *kaos* and *aporia.*

As if ancient Greek feelings were not enough, modern Greeks complicate matters even more with a range of unique and untranslatable Hellenic states of mind and emotion, from *meraki* to *derti,* included to show that you just can't keep a good Greek's feelings down.

eidolon [*ay*-doh-lon] (noun)

This term in Greek thought, meaning something like "image of a person" or "empty shadow" was what descended into

Hades after death as a shade or ghost. It did not indicate survival of an "immortal soul" in the sense that Western thought later arrived at. As we see from Homer's epic *The Odyssey* and other accounts of visiting Hades, the departed were literally "shadows of their former selves." The Greeks believed that two vital elements of the human being were lost at death, and one was *thymos*, a particularly difficult word to translate, but we'll have a shot at it below. The other was the life principle or something like consciousness, known as *psyche*. At death, this became a mere *eidolon*. The idea of *eidolon* explained for the Greeks why we sometimes see dead people in dreams or in dreamlike states. It has continued its meaning in the modern word "idol" with the same suggestion of "hollow image."

thymos [*thye*-mos] (noun)

This is the hardest of Greek words to translate, as we have no real equivalent in modern thought. Having said that, it has been argued that we should draw more on this quality in modern life in order to restore more "spiritedness" and shake us from our bourgeois contentment. The Greeks understood *thymos* to be the most active, willed element of the human being, situated somewhere around the diaphragm. It is easy to understand how early intuition arrived at this conclusion, as the ancient Chinese also found the *dan tien* or "energy center" in the same region of the body. At death, according to the Greeks, *thymos* simply vanished along with the *psyche,* leaving the *eidolon* or "empty shadow." Plato described *thymos* as that element of our nature where we feel pride, indignation, or shame, and it is through the *thymos* that we sacrifice ourselves for some cause, entirely against our own physical well-being. As political theorist Thomas G. Dineen writes, encouraging us to more *thymos:* "The person who swims into rough seas to rescue a stranger; the soldier who storms an enemy machine gun nest to save his mates; the fireman or policeman who risks his life to help those in peril – these people are living thymotically." I daresay it was out of an overactive *thymos* that arose the dubious quality denoted by the Greek *hubris,* which persuades a person that he can get away with almost anything he wants.

In biblical Greek, *thymos* is used to refer to the anger of God, mostly in the book of Revelation, where God's wrath is at its peak, both apoplectic and apocalyptic. In other biblical contexts we find divine anger more often given as the Greek word *orge,* a colder, more judgmental kind of disapproval that delivers its punishments without any cosmic fireworks.

aporia [ap-*aw*-ree-ah] (adjective)

Derived from *a-poros,* "no way through," this term refers to the feeling you get in almost any situation where you are at a loss, unable to work through a problem, cross a place, or reach a person. Indeed, this rather despairing state of mind has been described in its extreme form as "being radically at a loss before the world we inhabit." Anyone trying to drive through an unfamiliar city will have this feeling.

thambos [*tham*-bos] (noun)

Faced with nature in all its various aspects and moods, from its exquisite calmness to its most terrible extremes of violence,

ANCIENT AND CLASSICAL LANGUAGES

from its spectacular immensity to its tiniest and most detailed beauty, what are we to feel? Fear? Or joy? A sense of homage, awe, or respect? Whatever our feelings, they will be a curious blend of all these, and the Greeks had a word for it. *Thambos* summarizes all those mingled emotions that go with being struck dumb, literally "immobilized," by something way beyond one's understanding.

kaos [*kah*-os] (noun)

This resonant word has come down to us via Latin as "chaos," but this represents only one aspect of its original meaning. In Greek mythology, as recorded by Hesiod, creation in the form of three gods arose out of the void known as *Kaos,* which was itself a primordial godhead. Therefore, the term *kaos* meant a universe where there was nothing formed – a state of yawning nothingness, empty and hollow. The name comes from the Greek verb stem *kha*– meaning "to yawn" or "gape."

meraki [may-*rah*-kee] (adjective)

This is a word that modern Greeks often use to describe doing something with soul, creativity, or love – when you put "something of yourself" into what you're doing, whatever it may be. *Meraki* is often used to describe cooking or preparing a meal, but it can also mean arranging a room, choosing decorations, or setting an elegant table.

derti [*der*-tee] (adjective)

This is a troubled state of mind, maybe the result of some deep unhappiness that has to be conquered. Rather than rest in this pain, the Greek reaction is to try to burn your way out of it by throwing yourself passionately into life again.

kefi [*key*-fee] (adjective)

A word that says you're happy and just want to have a good time, enjoy good company over a good meal, drink, dance, and be merry. It's not a million miles removed from the Czech idea of *pohoda.*

Latin

Modern English has recourse to a whole lot of Latin terms and phrases that reveal the hugely significant inheritance of that language over the centuries, in rhetoric, philosophy, education, science, and law. Here are just a few: *a posteriori, a priori, ad hoc, cum laude, ex equo, honoris causa, mortis causa, rigor mortis, sancta sanctorum, vade retro, quid pro quo, curriculum vitae, alma mater.* Then we find another layer of phrases and terms corrupted or abbreviated from Latin, some no longer even recognizable. For example, *volle nolle* gave us "willy nilly," *QED* is short for *quod erat demonstrandum,* meaning literally, "it was to be proved," "to ad lib" comes from *ad libitum,* meaning, "as desired," *incognito* from "as unknown," *pro tem, A.M., P.M., versus, via, viz, et cetera, et cetera, et cetera.* We're speaking Latin all the time without knowing it!

However, we must delve into shadier reaches where meanings are not so obvious. And it becomes clear as we look further into their social habits that the Romans did nothing by halves.

gravitas [*grav*-ee-tas] (noun)

English borrowed this word from Latin, meaning "heaviness" – thus our word "gravity" – but gave it a fine meaning of someone who comes across with solemn or serious bearing. He who has *gravitas* is usually a teacher or public figure – and I say "he" with calculated trepidation as it is not a word commonly applied to women, however serious they may be. "Bush had to feign *gravitas,* Gore *veritas,*" said Jake Tapper in a quip about the American 2000 presidential election.

bacchanalia [bak-a-*nay*-lee-ah] (noun)

If you are going to celebrate the festival of the god of wine, *Bacchus,* there is surely only one way to do it – and that is by drinking a lot. In ancient times, *Bacchanalia* were celebrated in lower Italy by women only, probably as fertility rites. They

were at first secret, and held three times a year. Later they were introduced to Rome and men were admitted, upon which, as may be imagined, the general tenor declined. They became so popular that they became almost weekly events. Needless to say, the purple-stained mouths of revelers were also looking to celebrate the fertility aspect of such gatherings, and it seems the *Bacchanalia* became even more uninhibited than Carnival week in Rio. In 186 B.C. their appalling reputation led the Senate to issue an edict prohibiting unlicensed (literally) *Bacchanalia* throughout Italy.

accidia [ak-*see*-dee-ah] (noun)

This is a terrible state of spiritual torpor and sadness where one feels no desire or strength to act. It is sometimes written as *accidie*.

gynaeceum [gye-*nee*-see-um] (noun)

This has come down to us as a Latin word, but the Greeks thought of it first as *gunaikeion*, so we must give them the credit, too. The original term comes from the Greek *gune*, "a woman" – and thus our word gynaecology – and referred to the inner quarters of a house reserved for women, a practice continued by the Romans in their house design. In that sense, the Greek word is still used for the area of a Greek orthodox church where the women congregate separately from men during services. These days in feminist literature, *gynaeceum* has come to mean the social areas that were traditional domains of women rather than men and has acquired a negative ring of containment and separation rather than the original warmer associations of privacy and protection.

temulentia [tem-uh-*lent*-ee-ah] (noun)
An advanced apoplectic state of drunkenness, perhaps induced during *Bacchanalia*.

vomitarium [vom-ee-*tah*-ree-um] (noun)
This word always evokes Hollywood depictions of Roman meals, with Charles Laughton and accompanying cast reclining on couches, eating too much. It is the thoughtfully provided place where the Roman guest went to throw up in order to return to the table and indulge even longer. Nowadays it might be useful if pubs reintroduced the idea.

in flagrante [in flag-*rant*-ay] (idiom)
This word literally means "while the thing is blazing," but basically means that you are caught in the act of whatever you are doing. When a person is arrested *in flagrante delicto* the only evidence that is needed to convict him or her is to prove that fact. When someone is caught *in flagrante seducto* they have been caught with their pants down.

realia [ray-*ah*-lee-ah] (noun)
The word *realia* has its origins in Latin, but not the language spoken by the classical Romans, rather the medieval language of education, science, and philosophy. *Realia* means "real things," as opposed to words, which are neither "things" nor "real." Therefore it refers to objects and so requires the teacher or educator to put genuine articles or examples of things in front of a pupil, rather than simply to refer to them by using terms of vocabulary.

qualia [*kwah*-lee-ah] (noun)

This word's meaning could not be more opposed to *realia*. In philosophical jargon, *qualia* are those experiences that we cannot possibly describe in words, such as seeing a specific color. Whatever science says about colors being no more than reflected wavelengths in the light spectrum, try declaring that about a sunset or a red-light district and see the looks you get. Red is red is red, and therefore falls into the category of so-called *qualia*.

sub rosa [sub *roh*-zah] (idiom)

Literally, "under the rose," a lovely phrase with a long history. It is supposed to come from the gift of a rose, recorded in Greek myth, which Cupid made to the god of silence in return for keeping quiet about his mother Venus's many amours. Over time this gave rise to the practice of hanging a rose at meetings to indicate confidentiality, thus *sub rosa*, under the rose. The rose became a feature of the central boss of vaulted chambers as, for instance, a monastic chapter room where the community met, and was also placed over the confessional. In private houses, too, from Roman times onward, a decorative rose in the plasterwork of a dining-room ceiling indicated an assurance to guests of their host's discretion.

dulia [*doo*-lee-ah] (noun)

A Latin word again derived from the Greek *douleia*, meaning "service," which identifies the particular reverence and honor paid to angels and saints. This seems to be a theological distinction made in order to rebut the Reformation charge of worshipping saints as gods, as the Church struggled to distinguish between "worship" *(latria)* and "veneration" *(dulia)*.

Sanskrit

I n 1786, Sir William Jones, a British philologist and student of Ancient Indian, said the following about the Sanskrit language in an address to the Asiatick Society of Calcutta:

> The Sanskrit language is more perfect than the
> Greek, more copious than the Latin and more
> exquisitely refined than either, yet bearing to both
> of them a stronger affinity than could possibly have
> been produced by accident. So strong, indeed, that
> no philosopher could examine them all three,
> without believing them to have sprung from some
> common source which, perhaps, no longer exists.

Sanskrit certainly has entered English almost in an untranslated form because Western thought and spirituality has embraced the meanings as well as the words. Here is a selection of Sanskrit words that you might find almost familiar.

guru [*goo*-roo] (noun)

Guru in the modern Hindi and Punjabi languages now means "teacher," but it comes from the Sanskrit word *guruh*, which means "weighty," or "heavy," rather like the Latin word *gravitas*. It traditionally refers to a teacher or guide, especially in spiritual and philosophical matters. Now commonly used in the West, and we have our own less weighty version in "fitness guru."

nirvana [neer-*vah*-nah] (noun)

In Buddhism, this is a state of perfect happiness. It is the ineffable ultimate where one has attained disinterested wisdom and compassion. A transcendent state where there is no suffering, desire, or sense of self and the subject is released from the effects of karma. It represents the final

goal in Buddhism. Originally from the Sanskrit *nirva,* "be
extinguished," *nis,* "out," and *va,* "to blow."

yoga [*yoh*-gah] (noun)

Meaning "union," it refers to the union of the mind, body, and
spirit. This is a Hindu spiritual and ascetic discipline that
includes breath control, simple meditation, and the adoption
of specific body postures widely practiced for relaxation.

mantra [*man*-trah] (noun)

Generally known as a combination of syllables for meditation
or affirmations often found on *mani* wheels, one of the oldest
and best known mantras is the *om mane padme hum* of yogic
chanting. But *mantra* also has a deeper and more powerful

meaning. *Man–* means "mental," or "in mind," and *–tra* stands
for "a tool." So the word represents a verbal instrument for
mental imagery, a non–linguistic expression of the mind.

kamasutra [*kah*-mah-*soo*-trah] (noun)

Made popular by numerous Western books, marital therapists,
and psychologists, this is a Sanskrit treatise setting out rules for
sexual, sensuous, and sensual love and marriage in accordance
with Hindu law.

Gaelic

G aelic is an ancient Celtic tongue with an oral tradition that spans almost two thousand years and reflects a crofting lifestyle that remained virtually unchanged in all that time.

Sadly, much of this Scottish tradition was cruelly suppressed toward the end of the nineteenth century. Schoolchildren were chastised for speaking Gaelic, which was condemned as a pagan tongue. Old men and women were mocked for their charms, hymns, and incantations. Dance and song were banned. Musicians were forced to burn or hide their fiddles. The spirit of the *ceilidh* was broken.

Had it not been for the passionate enthusiasm of Alexander Carmichael, a wandering exciseman whose job took him around the Highlands and islands, practically all of the old lore would have been lost forever. His inspiring collection of Gaelic oral folklore, the *Carmina Gadelica,* was first published in 1900 and captures the spirit of a remarkable language and community aligned with nature and a culture almost unimaginably remote from that of the English and other Europeans.

He particularly captures the true depth of traditional meaning of the spirit of *ceilidh* in the following account:

> In a crofting community, the people work in unison in the field during the day, and discuss together in the house at night. This meeting is called *ceilidh* – a word that throbs the heart of the Highlander wherever he be. The *ceilidh* is a literary entertainment where stories and tales, poems and ballads are rehearsed and recited, and songs are sung, conundrums are put, proverbs are quoted, and many other literary matters are related and discussed. Let me briefly describe the *ceilidh* as I have seen it.

What follows is a touching and warm description of a village gathering in the storyteller's home, around the light of the peat fire in the middle of the floor. The people sit around, few hands being idle, as a woman spins, a man plaits a basket, and a girl cards, her wool. Others sew, embroider, or twist laths to hold down thatch. When the news of the day and the moods of the weather are dealt with, the storyteller is asked to perform. A tale can last an evening, or many, and when it is at last done, the audience sits and discusses the merits and demerits of the characters, before moving on to other entertainments.

Much has disappeared with those times, but the *ceilidh* still preserves its delightful character of being a gathering of the whole community, young and old, enjoying themselves together in a spontaneous way.

The Celtic language of this age-old tradition is permeated with untranslatables and, as the following examples show, with echoes of beliefs and customs that date back to the fourth or fifth centuries and the time of Saint Columba himself.

brác [brack] (noun)
A deer, but also with wonderful evocation. According to context it can be: the roar of a stag, the curve of an antler, or the curve of a wave immediately before breaking.

bialag [bee-*ah*-lak] (noun)
A person in front of another on horseback – such a useful word that it had to be included. But what isn't clear is whether this is the person driving or the passenger!

caim [*caym*] (noun)

The word means literally "a sanctuary." It's an imaginary circle made around the body with the hand. It serves as a ring of protection.

cailleach [*cal*-yak] (noun)

Literally "a woman," usually an old single woman, or even a nun, but the nearest sense would be "hag." However, in English this term is now corrupted with associations of witchcraft or supernatural and malign activity. In Celtic mythology, the *cailleach* is considered as the "crone" aspect of the Triple Goddess. In a telling metaphor, the cruel winds of early April, punishing the first green shoots of the year, are seen as the work of a wild *cailleach* or storm goddess who wields her switch against the young plants until finally giving up in disgust and disappearing till another season. Similarly around Halloween, the *cailleach* appears as the winter goddess bringing the first frosts. She is one who needs to be appeased. Traditionally, the first farmer to finish harvesting would make a corn-dolly or *cailleach* from the straw and pass it on to the next and so on until it came to the last farmer. This farmer was obliged to keep an eye on the "old woman" until the next year's harvest.

craic [*crak*] (noun)

"Where's the *craic?*" is the cry of any Irish person arriving in a new city. With an original meaning close to something like "chat," obviously essential to any Irish get-together, the term now means the combination of elements all adding up to a good time – fun, laughter, chatter, music, and warm company. Having the *craic,* or "enjoying yourself," is central to Irish life, and the phrase *ceoil agus craic,* which means "singing and a good time," says it all. Those of Irish blood, of course, who do nothing by halves, will insist not just on *craic* but on having "the good *craic!*"

sluagh [*sloo*-agh] (noun)

Literally, "the hosts of the departed." In Celtic mythology, the spirits of the departed continued the activities that they had most loved in the land of the living, especially hunting and fighting. Tales were told by those who had seen a vision of the hosts battling on a moonlit night or riding through the skies "with hounds on leash and hawks on hand" toward the farthest bournes beyond the seas.

sian [*shee*-ahn] (noun)

Soft and sorrowful music full of enchantment, which can be heard coming from a fairy knoll.

goisear [*gay*-ser] (noun)

This word has entered modern Scottish English as "guiser" and now refers simply to "carol singer." But in the old tradition, the *goisearan* were present at all the great festivals of the year and were a band of village youth dressed up with masked faces as kings, queens, bishops, and nuns. Making as much noise as possible, they brought blessings to every house in exchange for presents. Traditionally, these offerings were carried off in a lambskin bag known as *uilim* to a barn where the revelers then held a large feast and a dance and invited their girlfriends.

rèiteach [*ray*-ti-ok] (noun)

A gathering when a man would formally ask permission for a woman's hand in marriage from her father or next of kin. Over the years this event has become a more general "get together," but the word still retains the meaning of a kind of engagement party. One would say "At the *rèiteach*" or "Are you going to the *rèiteach?*" It is never translated into English, as there is no literal translation.

Chapter 9

Indigenous Languages

I t is easy to marvel at indigenous languages. They reflect how tiny cultures around the world, some cut-off for centuries from the invasive influence of powerful nations, sustain diverse and unique ways of seeing and understanding their world. Anthropologists have long found refreshment and inspiration in the purity and simplicity of so-called "primitive cultures." Nearly all indigenous cultures retain a spiritual awareness and respect for the natural world on which they depend for their survival. The surrounding environment is often seen as an appearance of a deeper interconnected reality in which humans and animals, plants, birds, and trees are all soul-fellows. Systems of worship and belief accompany these insights. Anthropologist Carlos Castaneda related a challenging account of his apprenticeship in Mexico with Don Juan, the Yaqui shaman. He uncovered a troubling world of which he never could have dreamed. For good or ill, the shaman has access to powerful forces underlying all nature. Don Juan speaks of the *nagual*, the invisible reality that lies behind all creation. "The *nagual* is the part of us for which there is no description – no words, no names, no feelings, no knowledge." Commentators use terms like "unspeakable" and "indescribable" for the *nagual*. Untranslatable? It would seem so.

Onto the Kalahari desert where the !Kung people (the ! indicates a pronunciation neither you nor I should attempt) divert the arrows of sickness, misfortune, or death fired at them by harmful spirits. To protect the people, their healers perform trance dances to awaken a strange force that they call *n/um*. The unpronounceable and untranslatable *n/um* sleeps in the base of the spine and once awoken climbs into the consciousness of the dancer and can be used to perform healing.

Mention the dilemma of untranslatable words to anybody and you can be sure they will recall the famous number of words that the Inuit people have for "snow." It makes sense, doesn't it, that people of the Arctic regions would have a lot to say about snow? Whereas there are many words for snow, there seem to be even more to describe "ice." Richard K. Nelson wrote of many types of ice in *Hunters of the Northern Ice*, including *uguruguzak, maullik, pogazak, mogozak, migalik,* and *salagok.* This final one you may have heard of. It is young black ice that is not thick enough to support a man and is weak enough to enable seals to break through with their heads to breathe.

R. M. W. Dixon in *The Languages of Australia* discusses the Indigenous Australian Yidiny dialect and its sensitivity to different kinds of noise. These include *dalmba,* "the sound of cutting," *mida,* "the noise of a person clicking his tongue against the roof of his mouth, or the noise of an eel hitting the water," *maral,* "the noise of hands being clapped together," *nyurrugu,* "the noise of talking heard a long way off when the words cannot quite be made out," *yuyurngal,* "the noise of a snake sliding through the grass," *ganga,* "the noise of some person approaching, for example, the sound of his feet on leaves or through the grass, or even the sound of a walking stick being dragged along the ground."

Here are some other words that help us get a glimpse at a culture behind the translation.

bol (Mayan, Mexico, and Honduras) [*bowl*] (noun, adjective)
There's nothing like telling things as they are – the Mayans of south Mexico and Honduras use the word *bol* for in-laws as well as stupidity! It translates as "stupid in-laws." Also, not very flatteringly, the root word for *bol* indicates a dazed befuddlement or stupor. Some things are universal and it seems that most cultures find it hard to cope with the in-laws.

hozh'q (Navajo, North America) [*hoe*-shk] (noun)
This means "the beauty of life, as seen and created by a person." For the Navajo, this is something that grows from within a human being and spreads outward to permeate the universe. It can be intellectual, emotional, moral, aesthetic, and biological. Navajo life and culture are very much based on this concept of *hozh'q,* and indeed the goal of life is the unity of experience. *Hozh'q* expresses ideas of order, happiness, health, and well-being as well as balance and harmony. Hence, it is not only a way of looking at life, but a way to live.

powwow (Algonquin, North America) [*pow*-wow] (noun)
Like the Indigenous Australian *corroboree,* this word originally referred only to a gathering of medicine men, coming together to perform a healing ceremony. Now it has come to mean a gathering of any kind of people and evokes an idea of talking and celebrating.

shima (Navajo, North America) [*shee*-mah] (noun)
This is a belief in the "earth as mother." The Native American spiritual beliefs regarded the planet as the literal mother of humankind. It echoes the figure of *Gaia,* who was the goddess of the earth in Greek creation mythology, a concept resurrected in our own time in the scientific insights of James Lovelock revealing the subtle checks and balances that maintain our planet's stability. Both *Gaia* and *Shima* express the idea that the earth itself is alive, an organic entity that must be respected. It's an appropriate time to introduce this Navajo word and belief into our language when modern industry, mines, and urban development are polluting the earth and air

of the Navajo ancestral lands. If we could remember that we humans are ourselves related parts of a complex and interconnected organism, we may perhaps begin to show more care for the world on which our lives depend.

kohanga reo (Maori, New Zealand) [koh-hang-ah *ray*-oh] (noun)

Many indigenous languages face extinction, particularly in places that are less isolated from the world and where the people of the language group are a minority group dying without passing on their knowledge. This is true of languages in places like Australia, North America, Canada, and New Zealand. *Kohanga reo* is the Maori effort to stop this from happening to their language. Literally translating as "language nest," this word refers to Maori-speaking preschools, where the language is actively being taught. Now more than 50 percent of the Maori speakers are under twenty-five years of age.

onsay (Boro, India) [*on*-say] (noun)

From one of the many Indigenous dialects of India, this is a language that adds various levels of meaning to the English word "love" that we must spell out if we wish to convey them. *Onsay* is Boro's concise way of saying "pretend to love." *Onguboy* more positively means "to love from the heart." *Onsra* has a level of sadness and translates as "to love for the last time."

billabong (Indigenous Australian) [*bil*-ah-bong] (noun)
This word is an Indigenous Australian term that has passed
into common usage in Australia but is quite untranslatable
when out of the context of the landscape. It is literally a
"branch of a river cut off from the main stream." The
term is well known due to the pseudo–Australian national
anthem and poem by Banjo Paterson, dating from the
1890s, *Waltzing Matilda*. This song is brimming with
untranslatables:

Oh there once was a swagman camped in the billabong
Under the shade of a Coolibah tree
And he sang as he looked at the old billy boiling
Who'll come a waltzing Matilda with me

Even the English language, from England to America to
Australia, has its fair share of untranslatables!

ngarong (Dyak, Borneo) [nn-*gam*-rawng] (noun)
Perhaps akin to Western ideas of spirit–guides, guardian
angels, or even little fairies or elves that come and make
shoes at night, a *ngarong* is an adviser that appears in a dream.
They are "dream–helpers" that distil an elusive idea and are
responsible for the feeling of clarification one sometimes gets
when they "sleep on something."

corroboree (Indigenous Australian) [co-*ro*-be-ree] (noun)
This word describes a traditional Aboriginal ceremony,
usually involving singing and dancing, often performed
at twilight. Many of these dances and ceremonies are
performed with special instruments, including the backing
of an Australian Aboriginal wind instrument called the
didgeridoo and various drums. As parts of these dances,
members of a tribe paint particular designs on their
bodies to indicate the type of ceremony being held and
the language group and family group performing. *Corroborees*
can have many meanings, from initiation ceremonies to secret
men's or women's business.

también de dolor se canta cuando llorar no se puede

(Aztec) [tam-bee-*yen* day *doh*-lor say *can*-tah *quan*-doh lyoh-*rar* noh say *pway*-day] (idiom)

This phrase captures something of the Portuguese *saudade* and means, similarly, "pain is also sung when crying isn't possible." It is about putting on a brave face, singing happy songs in the face of bitter sadness. Such songs both protect against and mask sorrow, something that the Mexican culture learned to do as heartbreak and hardship mark much of their history.

koyaanisqatsi (Hopi, North America) [coy-on-iss-*cot*-see] (noun)

The Hopi live in the oldest continuously inhabited community in North America and *koyaanisqatsi* means "life out of balance." It can also mean "a life that is so crazy that it calls for a new way of living." The crazy pace of life in some big cities, especially at rush hour, is definitely *koyaanisqatsi*; if you've been staying up all weekend, have had very little sleep and it's now Monday morning, it's also certainly *koyaanisqatsi*.

mokita (Kiriwina, New Guinea) [moe-*kee*-tah] (noun)

A powerful word used to describe the truth that everyone knows but no one wants to talk about openly. This unspoken truth is usually something unpleasant or unwelcome that will disrupt the social peace or bring perceived family embarrassment if brought into the open.

mamihlapinatapei (Tierra del Fuego) [*mam*-i-lah-pi-na-ta-*pay*-ee] (noun)

You know when *mamihlapinatapei* has just happened. It is that look across the table or the room when two people are sharing a private and unspoken moment. When each knows the other understands and is in agreement with what is being expressed. It may be a romantic moment but equally can be a moment of humor or forgiveness. A delightfully untranslatable word to describe an expressive and meaningful silence.

Chapter 10

Creole and Pidgin Languages

O ver two hundred varieties of Creole and pidgin languages have been documented around the world, from Polynesia to the Caribbean, from Mauritius to Louisiana. Long dismissed as mere corruptions of mainstream languages, they now receive great interest as fascinating elements in the archaeology of global language development.

Creole is seen as distinctive from pidgin, more developed grammatically, richer in its borrowings, and usable in a much wider set of social situations. Some Creole forms even have a literature, as in Haiti, for instance, where the majority of the population are Creole-speakers.

The word "Creole" itself comes from the Portuguese *crioulo,* or *criolo,* referring (usually) to a black child born in the household of a master, distinguishing them from those born in their native Africa. The origin of the word "pidgin" is more doubtful, with a number of theories running into each other. Some see it as a Chinese corruption of the English word "business," dating from early trading contacts along the China Sea. Others trace it to the name of a South American tribe with whom Europeans had trading links. Some find its origin in a Jewish argot known as *pidyom* found in eighteenth-century London. What is clear is that the term goes back two or three centuries at least. It refers to a kind of basic interlanguage, stripped of grammatical complexities.

Some fantastically colorful and culture-specific phrases come out of Creole and pidgin cultures. One such phrase, *pic so orite,* literally means "to poke the octopus." What on earth could this mean? Something positive, of course, akin to "go for it" or "rise to the challenge" in English.

In some cases, like Jamaican *patois* where significant remnants of African languages were brought over to the plantations, the range of the language borrowings is wide and complex.

One of my favorite Jamaican terms, which comes from Rastafarian culture, is *ital,* a word in itself meaning no more than "without salt" but with a wonderful depth of association. Rastafarians have a strict diet code that excludes salt, and they insist not only upon pure ingredients but also ideally on eating meals prepared by their own hands. *Ital* food is therefore food that meets these strict requirements and is "pure" in every sense. By extension it refers to any product that is pure, such as the "high-grade" marijuana intrinsic to Rasta culture. If it is *ital,* you know it's the best, natural grown "seeds and all" weed.

Most indigenous cultures have their mysterious and wonderful beliefs in the supernatural. They can range from the scary but probably harmless *duppy* of Jamaica to the more insidious *dorlis* of the Antilles. And, last but not least, the truly awful *zonbi* of Haitian *vodun,* long absorbed as the word "voodoo" into horror film mythology. Whatever the truth behind such lurid traditions, the colorful and frequently untranslatable character of Caribbean and other local cultures will endure undiminished for a long time.

kilim (Tok Pisin) [*ki*-lim] (verb)

It is generally understood that pidgin words mean in English exactly as they sound. Beware this word *kilim*. To the English ear, this sounds like a command to "kill him." This word, while it does incite violence, would not precede a murder! It means to hit someone, and to hit them hard. If someone was commanding you to kill, they would say *kilim i dai*.

ti pouchon (Haitian Creole) [*tee* poo-chone] (noun)

This word might find itself in heavy use at bars in the Western world. It refers to a very handsome young man who is also wealthy. Just being good-looking isn't enough to be considered *ti pouchon*.

kiasu (Singlish) [kee-*a*-soo] (noun)

The word *kiasu* comes from Hokkien. It means "always wanting the best for oneself and trying hard to get it." The *kiasu* student is always the first to get the book out of the library – they may even hide the book in the wrong shelf so that no one else can read it – and always the first to get their assignments in to the teacher. At a buffet the *kiasu* person may be so concerned that the restaurant will run out of oysters that they dish all the oysters onto their plate, to make sure they will get enough. *Kiasu*-ism is a keenness that might be mildly exploitative. This has been adopted in Singapore, in a spirit of self-mockery, as a national characteristic, and I think the word can be said to have passed into the local vocabulary!

bel hevi (Tok Pisin) [bel *heh*-vi] (noun)

This word literally translates as "belly heavy" and refers to that heavy sinking feeling that often accompanies extreme sadness.

potlatch (Chinook Jargon) [*pot*-latch] (noun)

Some North American Indian peoples hold a big ceremonial feast called *potlatch*. Here possessions are given away or destroyed to display the wealth of the giver and to enhance their prestige. It's an "I've got so much, I can afford to give it away" type of behavior.

wantok (Tok Pisin) [*wahn*-tok] (noun)

This word encompasses your clanspeople, relatives, people from your village, even from your country. Literally translatable as one who speaks the same language, "one talk," it is someone who now has some claim on you. You belong to the village and the village has some responsibility to you and you to it.

garam (Singlish) [gah-*ram*] (noun)

Singaporeans have borrowed this word, *garam,* which translates literally as "salt," from the Malay language. However, it doesn't mean "salt" in Singlish. A Singaporean might say "I'm so *garam* with you," which roughly means "I can't stop thinking of you" but includes the gesture of actually hugging someone. An example perhaps of a word that has transcended translatability and has come to mean something else.

Word Finder

IN OTHER WORDS

First published in the United States of America in 2004 by
Walker Publishing Company, Inc., by arrangement with
Elwin Street Limited.

Conceived and produced by Elwin Street Limited
79 St John Street
London EC1M 4NR
www.elwinstreet.com

Editor: Erin King
Illustrator: Neil Packer
Designer: Sharanjit Dhol

For information about permission to reproduce selections from
this book, write to Permissions, Walker & Company,
104 Fifth Avenue, New York, New York 10011.

Library of Congress Cataloging-in-Publication Data
available upon request
ISBN 0-8027-1444-7

Visit Walker & Company's Web site at www.walkerbooks.com

Printed in China

2 4 6 8 10 9 7 5 3 1